Praise for
The Nurse Manager's Guide
to Budgeting & Finance, 2nd Edition

" CNOs are responsible for ensuring their nursing leadership teams understand how the decisions they make on a daily basis impact organizational finances and quality of care. In *The Nurse Manager's Guide to Budgeting & Finance*, 2nd Edition, Al Rundio provides exemplars for crucial leadership development and successful fiduciary knowledge on your nursing team. Armed with this knowledge, nurses will be empowered to lead your organization with contemporary financial acumen and practice. Both editions will become staples in your nursing leadership library. Once you read this book, you will wonder how you survived without these tools in your toolbox. "

–Joanne O. Miller, DNP, RN, NEA-BC
Chief Nursing Officer/Vice President Patient Care Services
Sibley Memorial Hospital/Johns Hopkins Medicine

" Nurse leaders are uniquely positioned to deliver revenue maximization and improved clinical outcome results demanded by healthcare reform. A comprehensive understanding of budgeting is imperative to fulfill this major accountability. In this edition of *The Nurse Manager's Guide to Budgeting & Finance*, Rundio provides a budgeting context in his new chapters on healthcare reform, organizational governance, and QSEN competencies and has updated his clear, concise guide to clinical financial management. Required reading for nurse leaders. "

–Donald T. Wenzler, DNP, MBA, RN, NEA-BC
Chief Nursing Officer
Antelope Valley Hospital

" This second edition of *The Nurse Manager's Guide to Budgeting & Finance* is an essential book for nursing students, professionals, and managers alike because it addresses financial issues nurse managers regularly encounter. Often, nursing students and professional nurses are catapulted into manager positions without the necessary knowledge and skills in the financial area where they are expected to function. This edition covers a broad range of topics related to healthcare finance, including accounting, budgeting, and reimbursement issues, as well as new chapters on the Affordable Care Act, healthcare governing boards, and quality and safety issues that nurse leaders deal with regularly. A 'must-have' guide for all nurses who have administrative responsibilities, this book is full of down-to-earth, real-life examples that help nurses better understand financial management. I guarantee that you will use this book often as you maneuver through your administrative duties. "

–*William J. Lorman, JD, PhD, MSN, RN*
Vice President & Chief Clinical Officer
Livengrin Foundation, Inc.

" The leadership competencies needed in today's healthcare market are fundamentally different from what many nurses learned in the past. Al Rundio has provided a comprehensive, succinct, and contemporary perspective that supports the needed learnings of present-day nurse leaders. *The Nurse Manager's Guide to Budgeting & Finance*, 2nd Edition, should be required reading for all nurse managers and directors. "

–*Michelle Conley, MBA, BSN, RN, CENP*
Senior Vice President and Chief Nursing Officer
Aria Health

the NURSE MANAGER'S GUIDE to BUDGETING & FINANCE

2nd ED.

Al Rundio, PhD, DNP, RN, APRN, NEA-BC, FNAP, FIAAN, FAAN

Sigma Theta Tau International
Honor Society of Nursing®

Sigma Theta Tau International
Honor Society of Nursing®

The Honor Society of Nursing, Sigma Theta Tau International (STTI) is a nonprofit organization founded in 1922 whose mission is advancing world health and celebrating nursing excellence in scholarship, leadership, and service. Members include practicing nurses, instructors, researchers, policymakers, entrepreneurs, and others. STTI's roughly 500 chapters are located at approximately 700 institutions of higher education throughout Armenia, Australia, Botswana, Brazil, Canada, Colombia, England, Ghana, Hong Kong, Japan, Kenya, Lebanon, Malawi, Mexico, the Netherlands, Pakistan, Portugal, Singapore, South Africa, South Korea, Swaziland, Sweden, Taiwan, Tanzania, Thailand, the United Kingdom, and the United States. More information about STTI can be found online at http://www.nursingsociety.org.

Sigma Theta Tau International
550 West North Street
Indianapolis, IN, USA 46202

To order additional books, buy in bulk, or order for corporate use, contact Nursing Knowledge International at 888.NKI.4YOU (888.654.4968/US and Canada) or +1.317.634.8171 (outside US and Canada).

To request a review copy for course adoption, email solutions@nursingknowledge.org or call 888. NKI.4YOU (888.654.4968/US and Canada) or +1.317.634.8171 (outside US and Canada).

To request author information, or for speaker or other media requests, contact Marketing, Honor Society of Nursing, Sigma Theta Tau International at 888.634.7575 (US and Canada) or +1.317.634.8171 (outside US and Canada).

ISBN: 9781940446585
EPUB ISBN: 9781940446592
PDF ISBN: 9781940446608
MOBI ISBN: 9781940446615

Library of Congress Cataloging-in-Publication Data
Names: Rundio, Al, author. | Sigma Theta Tau International, publisher.
Title: The nurse manager's guide to budgeting & finance / Al Rundio.
Other titles: Nurse manager's guide to budgeting and finance
Description: Second edition. | Indianapolis, IN: Sigma Theta Tau
   International, [2016] | Includes bibliographical references.
Identifiers: LCCN 2015048653 (print) | LCCN 2015049139 (ebook) | ISBN
   9781940446585 (print : alk. paper) | ISBN 9781940446592 (epub : alk.
   paper) | ISBN 9781940446608 (pdf : alk. paper) | ISBN 9781940446615 (mobi
   : alk. paper) | ISBN 9781940446592 (Epub) | ISBN 9781940446608 (Pdf) |
   ISBN 9781940446615 (Mobi)
Subjects: | MESH: Economics, Nursing | Budgets | Nurse Administrators
Classification: LCC RT86.7 (print) | LCC RT86.7 (ebook) | NLM WY 77 | DDC
   362.17/3068--dc23
LC record available at http://lccn.loc.gov/2015048653

First Printing, 2016
Publisher: Dustin Sullivan
Acquisitions Editor: Emily Hatch
Editorial Coordinator: Paula Jeffers
Cover Designer: Katy Bodenmiller
Interior Design/Page Layout: Katy Bodenmiller

Principal Book Editor: Carla Hall
Development Editor: Keith Cline
Copy and Project Editor: Kevin Kent
Proofreader: Dwight Ramsey
Indexer: Larry D. Sweazy

Dedication

This book is dedicated to my sister, Phyllis Rundio Lopez, and her family—husband Ralph and children Andrew and Abigail. They are a constant presence in my life and are there for me whenever I need to call on them. Their understanding and love truly demonstrate what family is all about.

Acknowledgments

I acknowledge everyone who has been on my journey as a nurse and nurse leader. Their guidance and mentorship have led me where I am today in healthcare and nursing. There are so many individuals that to name them all would be impossible. So, this acknowledgment goes out to all of those individuals. They know who they are.

I also want to acknowledge the International Nurses Society on Addictions. I had the opportunity to lead this organization from 2012 to 2014. As with any leadership opportunity, one learns with every endeavor. I am most grateful and appreciative to my executive committee: Dana Murphy-Parker, MSN, RN, PMHNP, CARN-AP, president-elect; William J. Lorman, JD, PhD, RN, PMHNP, CARN-AP, FIAAN, treasurer; and Dennis Hagarty, MSN, RN, CARN, secretary. I also am very grateful to our new management company, Prime Management, and our executive director, Robert Ranieri, MBA. I had the opportunity to change management companies my last year of office, and I could not have accomplished this without these individuals.

I also want to acknowledge the individuals that I work most closely with at Drexel University College of Nursing and Health Professions: Faye Meloy, PhD, RN, associate dean for pre-licensure nursing programs; Anna Pohuly and Fred Anderson, assistants to the associate deans; and Gloria Ferraro Donnelly, PhD, RN, FAAN, dean of the College of Nursing and Health Professions.

About the Author

Al Rundio, PhD, DNP, RN, APRN, NEA-BC, FNAP, FIAAN, FAAN, is an experienced clinician, administrator, and educator. He is the associate dean for post-licensure nursing programs & CNE and clinical professor of nursing at Drexel University College of Nursing and Health Professions in Philadelphia, Pennsylvania. He is the former vice president of nursing/CNO at Shore Medical Center, Somers Point, New Jersey. He is a member of the board of trustees, Inspira Health System, Joint Hospital Board in New Jersey. Rundio practices part time as a nurse practitioner in a residential addictions treatment center. He is the immediate past president of the International Nurses Society on Addictions. Rundio is coauthor of the *Nurse Executive Review and Resource Manual,* first and second editions, published by the American Nurses Credentialing Center. He also is coeditor and coauthor of *The Doctor of Nursing Practice and the Nurse Executive Role,* published by Wolters Kluwer Health. He is a popular speaker on nurse manager and leadership topics.

Table of Contents

Foreword

Nursing is a blend of art and science. This is especially true when referring to the role of the nurse manager. This is one of the most pivotal roles in the nursing department, where managers have accountability for patient and staff satisfaction, quality and clinical outcome measures, human resource management, supply management, unit operations, staff retention and development, and a host of other responsibilities. In the middle of all that juggling, managers are challenged to accomplish these responsibilities in a fiscally sound manner.

With the exception of dealing with staffing and schedules, budget management is a manager's biggest challenge. Budget managers must forecast, design, build, manage, and analyze their budgets. Although each organization has a unique budgeting process, there are basics that every nurse manager must understand. Typically, managers have very good clinical skills but sometimes struggle with financial acumen. Therein lies the gap.

The Nurse Manager's Guide to Budgeting & Finance, 2nd Edition, bridges that gap! Author Al Rundio provides a strong foundation for the novice and even some challenging examples for experienced managers. I have used this book in both hospital and academic settings. Managers find the information builds on their current knowledge base and use it as a reference when budget time rolls around. Students at both the master's and doctorate levels find this book a strong basis for assignments and case studies. The valuable information enables the nurse leader to understand and negotiate budgets. Mastering this information also contributes to nurse leaders attaining some of the tenets of the Institute of Medicine's 2010 report *The Future of Nursing: Leading Change, Advancing Health.* Nurse leaders are able to work at the highest level of their education and training, develop collaborative relationships related to finance and healthcare costs.

This book is a must read for nursing leaders. I am proud to recommend this work and am confident that you will find it a welcome addition to your personal leadership library.

–Ann Marie Papa, DNP, RN
Chief Nursing Officer, Einstein Health System

Introduction

Many nurses become nurse managers as the next necessary step to advance their careers, some from a desire to contribute to nurses and nursing within their organization. Oftentimes, nurses find themselves in a management position without the tools and skills needed to do the job effectively. As revenue decreases in most healthcare facilities, more pressure is placed on nurse managers to manage the organization's resources (both human capital and supplies) more judiciously. All of a sudden, words like "productivity" and "staffing to census" have become the norm. In order to manage the organization's resources more wisely, nurse managers must be armed with the necessary tools to do the job well.

This book is written with the nurse manager in mind at the unit level and above for any healthcare organization. There is no question that our past dictates our future, and the reality is that healthcare is a business. With decreasing revenue streams, nurse managers must possess some basic knowledge about budgeting and finance. The reality is that each nurse manager is managing his or her own business (the nursing unit) within the organization.

With decreasing revenue streams, nurse managers must manage their units so that actual expenses equal budgeted expenses. This can be a difficult task for many nurse managers. Nurse managers must be able to justify variances and take corrective action where needed. Nurse managers must also be familiar with certain types of budget reports, how to interpret these reports, and, most importantly, how to take action to control the results.

This book is a handbook that is intended to be used on the job for the effective management of the organization's finances. It is also intended to provide the nurse manager with concepts that can be implemented in management, so that the nurse manager becomes more effective at managing the resources of the organization.

The United States of America, this book's primary audience, is unique compared to many other countries, especially those that have a national single-payer health plan. The United States has numerous insurance products on the market, and U.S. citizens generally receive health benefits from their employers, which are subsidized by the employee. Some individuals purchase an entire insurance product on their own. The elderly and certain patient populations—such as dialysis patients—receive Medicare. The poor can receive Medicaid. The Children's Health Insurance Program (CHIP) covers otherwise uninsured children. Medicare and Medicaid are the two federal programs of insurance for healthcare. Although the United States does not have a single-payer, federally funded system, it is important to emphasize that national single-payer systems also have financial problems sometimes equal to or greater than the United States'. A free-market system, like the system we have in the United States, creates competition. Such competition can lower rates, as well as add services and products.

The reality in the United States is that healthcare costs continue to rise. Many of these costs are related to unnecessary tests and procedures. Insured Americans are experiencing tighter controls from insurance plans, where second and third opinions for certain elective procedures may be required, and where certain medications need approval from the insurance company. The other reality that was facing the United States was the estimated 42 million Americans with no health insurance. The Patient Protection and Affordable Care Act has helped to address this problem through insurance exchanges and financial penalties if an uninsured person does not purchase a health insurance plan. The number of Americans with no health insurance creates one type of access problem: If the person is not insured, that person may not seek healthcare when needed and may not seek primary care for prevention of illness. As more Americans are obtaining healthcare insurance, another type of access problem can be potentially created. This access problem relates to the number of primary care providers, which is not sufficient to serve more insured. Thus, long delays to access health services will most likely be the end result. Advanced practice nurses are in a pivotal position at this time: They should seize the moment to be the primary care providers of the nation. The Institute of Medicine's report on *The Future of Nursing* (2010) addresses this where the report calls for all nurses to function to their full scope of practice.

The uniqueness of healthcare reimbursement in the U.S. and the fact that we are the most industrialized country in the world that does not provide universal healthcare to all citizens place nurse managers in a pivotal position where they must balance cost with quality. To effectively do this, there is no doubt that nurse managers must understand the basic concepts of budgeting, which is the essence of this book for the nurse manager.

The second edition of *The Nurse Manager's Guide to Budgeting & Finance* takes a deeper dive into the nursing budget than the first edition. New information includes key legislation that is currently affecting finance and the nursing budget. The two major pieces of legislation addressed are the Medicare Modernization Act of 2003 and the Patient Protection and Affordable Care Act of 2010. Additional information is provided on value-based purchasing and accountable care organizations. Population-based healthcare is also discussed.

A new chapter on the Quality and Safety Education for Nurses (QSEN) competencies for graduate nursing education and their relationship to budgeting and finance has been developed. With the national initiative to have 10,000 nurses appointed to boards, a new chapter has been added on a board's fiduciary responsibility in providing oversight of an organization's budget. Looking into a crystal ball, a forecast for the future of finance and budgeting is provided.

Key chapter information is as follows:

Chapter 1, "Budgeting for the Nurse Manager," has additional information on not-for-profit and for-profit hospitals and healthcare systems.

Chapter 2, "Healthcare Reimbursement," includes a significant amount of material on the political history of healthcare reimbursement in the United States. The Medicare Prescription Drug, Improvement, and Modernization Act of 2003 is also thoroughly discussed.

Chapter 3, "Budget Types," includes additional information on the accrual basis of accounting, the cash basis of accounting, assets, liability, and equity. A specialty organization's balance sheet is utilized as an example of assets and liability. Responsibility center budgeting is also discussed in this chapter.

Chapter 4, "Budget Development," includes an additional section on inventory management.

Chapter 5, "Building Operating Budgets," takes a deeper dive into key concepts in the development of an operating budget. Information on performance management has been added. Gross and net patient service revenue as well as productive and nonproductive nursing hours are further defined with new examples. A new section on outpatient reimbursement has also been added.

Chapter 6, "Capital Budgets," now includes an example of equipment depreciation.

Chapter 7, "Budget Variances," has no changes because the concept of variance analysis has remained the same since the last edition of the book.

Chapter 8, "Budget Reports," has updated information in the examples of reports.

Chapter 9, "Healthcare Reform and the Affordable Care Act," is a new chapter that covers the Patient Protection and Affordable Care Act of 2010; this act is having a major impact on how healthcare is delivered and financed.

Chapter 10, "Governing Boards & Specialty Organizations," is a new chapter that covers governing boards. The American Academy of Nursing and several other nursing organizations are calling for 10,000 nurses to be appointed to boards of various types of organizations. The fiduciary responsibility of boards is discussed.

Chapter 11, "QSEN Competencies and High-Reliability Organizations," is a new chapter that covers QSEN and how quality relates to finance. High-reliability organizations are also discussed.

Chapter 12, "Conclusions," has added a section on communication because communication is a major factor in the performance of any organization, especially where financial matters are concerned.

Case examples have been added to a number of the chapters to further demonstrate the concepts being presented. These should assist you in further learning the principles of budgeting and finance.

References

Institute of Medicine (IOM). (2010). *The future of nursing: Leading change, advancing health*. Washington, DC: National Academies Press.

1

Budgeting for the Nurse Manager

My first nurse manager job was in an urban emergency department. In this hospital, the director of nursing generated and monitored the budget. The nurse manager never received budget reports or audits. In fact, nurse managers in this organization had no clue as to what constituted the budget, nor did they know whether they were over budget, under budget, or if the budget was balanced.

One day, the assistant director of nursing advised me that I was over budget and should do a better job of controlling overtime. The problem was not only did I have no idea we were over budget, but we were also short-staffed! In other words, I had accountability and responsibility but no real authority, all because the director of nursing controlled the budget. The moral of this story: If you are a nurse manager and are expected to manage a budget, you need to be part of the budgeting process.

Yin Yang: The Budget Process for Nurse Managers and the Relationship to Patient Care

Of course, many nurses are happy to avoid the nitty-gritty accounting details inherent in the development and management of a budget. This head-in-the-sand attitude with regard to financial affairs is perhaps understandable. After all, we went into nursing to care for patients. But what many of us often fail to remember is that caring for patients requires prioritizing need and allocating finite resources, which require budgeting.

Budgeting and finance are topics that are not addressed adequately in the typical nursing curriculum. This is understandable because nurses need to learn many things about clinical care, and so the curriculum focuses on that. Nurses get more exposure to finance and budgeting at the master's degree level, and those who pursue a nursing management degree learn the most about these topics.

"If you are a nurse manager and you are expected to manage a budget, you need to be part of the budgeting process."

A lot of nurses think that it is up to the nurse manager on the unit to worry about and manage the budget. However, the reality is that every item that we use has a cost associated with it that affects the budget—and thus the dollars—of the organization. You'd have to be living in a vacuum to miss how the general economy has affected your own life; the same is true in healthcare. There is not a bottomless pit of money and reimbursement. As my mom always said, "Money does not fall off trees."

Every nurse and other hospital employee must be accountable for the use of resources. Nurses who understand the budget process will be able to contribute positively to organizational performance and ensure the sustainability of their organizations.

Besides, although understanding financial and budgeting concepts can be challenging, it can also be fun. I challenge everyone to become well versed on these topics. After all, nursing is many professions rolled into one—and fiscal management should not be excluded.

> **NOTE**
>
> *In today's healthcare environment, managers are held accountable for the financial performance of their units. As President Harry Truman stated so well, "The buck stops here." At the same time, managers must have the authority and resources to carry out the functions for that unit.*

For-Profit Versus Nonprofit Healthcare Organizations

Before beginning our budgeting journey, it's important for you to understand the distinctions between the two major types of healthcare organizations: nonprofit organizations and for-profit organizations.

Most nurses today are employed in nonprofit hospitals or health systems. The history of healthcare sheds light on why. Originally, hospitals were charity organizations for providing care to dying patients. Care was free. As hospitals provided care to the communities that they served, hospitals initially were nonprofit to maintain tax-exempt status since they were providing care to a community of patients. However, since the 1990s an increase in for-profit hospitals and health systems has occurred.

So, about now, you're probably wondering: How do nonprofit healthcare organizations differ from those that are for-profit? The major differences as reported by the Centers for Medicare & Medicaid Services are as follows:

- A nonprofit hospital implies that the facility does not pay state or local property taxes or federal income taxes. The rationale for this is that the organization is considered a charity, and provides certain community benefits in accord with state and federal guidelines.

- A for-profit hospital or health system implies that the facility is either owned by private investors or is owned publicly by shareholders. The organization is part of a company that issues shares of stock to raise revenue to expand the hospital or health system's activities. (Free Management Library, n.d.)

Typically, for-profit hospitals have been based in the southern part of the United States, generally in Florida and Texas. For example, Hospital Corporation of America (HCA) was a large for-profit health system in Florida and other parts of the southern United States. Investor-owned hospitals have expanded nationally. Often, these hospital systems have purchased financially distressed facilities or stand-alone hospitals that are in need of access to capital for expansion. Depending on prevailing economic conditions, for-profit hospitals can gain better access to capital than nonprofit hospitals that expand by issuing debt through tax-exempt bonds.

The Congressional Budget Office (CBO) found that "on average, nonprofit hospitals provided higher levels of uncompensated care than did otherwise similar for-profit hospitals. Among individual hospitals, however, the provision of uncompensated care varied widely, and the distributions for nonprofit and for-profit hospitals largely overlapped. Nonprofit hospitals were more likely than otherwise similar for-profit hospitals to provide certain specialized services but were found to provide care to fewer Medicaid-covered patients as a share of their total patient population. On average, nonprofit hospitals were found to operate in areas with higher average incomes, lower poverty rates, and lower rates of uninsurance than for-profit hospitals" (CBO, 2006).

When we are reviewing hospitals and health systems, the differences between for-profit and nonprofit hospitals or health systems can be difficult to ascertain. There have also been some assumptions that hospital boards in for-profit health systems have more "insiders" appointed to the board rather than community members. It is also an assumption that for-profit hospitals and health systems will respond more quickly for financial incentives. One example is a for-profit hospital offering open-heart surgery rather than psychiatric or addiction services because the former reimburses at a significantly higher rate than the latter.

The reality is that as cost-containment becomes more critical and resources more restrained, many stand-alone hospitals will need to merge with larger systems, some of which will most certainly be for-profit health systems.

What Is a Budget?

Before you can explore the finer points of budgeting, it's critical to answer this question: What is a budget? A *budget* is all of the following:

- A forecast of the resources required to deliver the services offered by the organization

- A plan for coordinating the financial goals of an organization

- A formal, quantitative expression of management's plans, intentions, expectations, and actions to control results

The primary purpose of budgeting is to control costs. A budget is based on an organization's mission and strategic plan. If the budget is forecasted properly—which involves comprehensive data assessment—the actual outcomes will come close to the predicted outcomes.

> **NOTE**
>
> *A key aspect of the nurse manager's job is to achieve the goals and objectives of the organization. Today, that involves meeting those goals and objectives in a cost-effective manner.*

The budget process has three primary objectives:

- To establish an annual and a monthly budget
- To identify and analyze actual experience compared to the budget plan
- To accurately report all financial and statistical data

The Benefits of Budgeting

The budgeting process is essential to a well-functioning organization. The budget provides a forecast of what will occur, generally for a one-year time frame. It is a quantitative expression of management's plans, intentions, and actions. It really quantifies the strategic goals of the organization.

Accordingly, the budget process is not an optional endeavor. An investment of time in a well-planned budget will yield a future return on investment, that is, to sustain and maintain the viability of the organization. Once they are created, budgets get communicated to all key stakeholders so that everyone is on the same page. Although managers are held accountable for the budget process as well as monitoring operations to assure compliance with the budget, all staff must be held accountable to contribute to budget performance through the judicious use of supplies and labor.

Benefits of budgeting include the following:

- **Budgeting places everyone on the management team.** The one common denominator that every department manager in an organization must develop and use is the budget. Each departmental budget builds to the overall organizational budget. All managers are held accountable for their budget performance. One goal of any organization, whether nonprofit or for-profit, is to make a profit off of operations.

- **Budgeting helps to create cost awareness.** Budgeting is the formal, quantitative expression of management's plans and attentions. By paying attention to numbers, a greater cost awareness within the organization is created.

> *"Budgeting produces cost savings because the process creates cost awareness."*

- **Budgeting helps to measure individual and departmental productivity, as well as profitability.** All nurse managers must consider their responsibility center as their own business. The goal of any business, be it a for-profit or a nonprofit business, is to make money off of operations. Many hospitals and healthcare facilities have closed in our nation because of poor business and management practices. Every nurse manager must recognize that they manage a business. They must strive to make the business survive. This means that the business must be profitable.

- **Budgeting can produce cost savings.** Cost savings result because budgets force managers to justify every cost, expense, and revenue. It can make one aware that alternatives can exist that are more cost-effective. Simply put, budgeting produces cost savings because the process creates cost awareness.

- **Budgeting can help to reduce waste.** As cost awareness increases, nurse managers will focus on what costs can be reduced or eliminated, thus reducing waste in the organization.

- **Budgeting helps to minimize operational surprises.** These include cash shortages, operating losses, and so on. Operational surprises are eliminated because the budget creates a plan for expenses. One CEO I knew never assessed the needs of surgeons regarding capital equipment (major movable equipment) requests. His feeling was that surgeons always wanted expensive devices, so it was best not to ask. I felt the opposite. At budget-preparation time, I always sent a memo to each surgical department chief to ask what their capital budget needs were for the following year. That way, I knew what to budget for. This significantly minimized operational surprises, where midyear, a surgeon would suddenly request a $100,000 piece of equipment that was not in the budget.

- **Budgeting provides all levels of management with a set of predetermined operating standards with which to evaluate performance.** Budgeting places all managers on the same page, so to speak. Even though each department has different budget requirements, certain items remain standard across all departments (for example, across-the-board raises for employees and the percentage costs of employee benefits). The budget must tie directly to the organizational goals and objectives. The budget is the process that enables these goals and objectives to be achieved. By going through the budget process, managers are then aware of these organizational goals and objectives.

> *"If first-line nurse managers develop, in collaboration with finance, a well-thought-out budget, and if they implement and monitor it well and take corrective action when necessary, the facility will run like a smooth-sailing ship."*

- **Budgeting serves as an excellent means of educating and developing nurse managers.** How true this is! The best education for budgeting, fiscal management, and fiscal accountability comes from the finance department in the nurse manager's organization. The finance department for the hospital where I was a chief nursing officer (CNO) taught me a lot about fiscal management. I learned terms such as *in the aggregate* (the big picture), *amortization*, and so on. I had learned about financial management of healthcare facilities in college, but to actually live and breathe it is what really educated me about fiscal management. I relished working with our financial department, the budget manager, and the chief financial officer (CFO). They provided me with an education that has made me unafraid of budgets and finance. (My personal financial situation is healthy, too, thanks to what they taught me.)

- **Budgeting frees top management so that they can concentrate on developing strategies for future institutional growth.** It is up to all levels of managers to manage the budget. However, it is really the first-line manager or the nurse manager at the unit level who needs to do the most with budgeting. (Let's face it: They do the most with everything.) If first-line nurse managers develop, in collaboration with finance, a well-thought-out budget, and if they implement and monitor it well and take corrective action when necessary, the facility will run like a smooth-sailing ship. This also frees up top executives in the organization to concentrate on what they need to do (for example, develop a good strategic plan to keep the organization alive and thriving; develop and play a role in health policy, especially where reimbursement from federal and state programs is concerned; and so on).

For nurse managers, specifically, budgeting offers the following benefits:

- Forces a nurse manager to think ahead.

- Compels a nurse manager to make choices.

- Provides a plan or forecast of what is expected.

- Provides for communication within the organization.

- Provides a basis for evaluation and control.

- Helps clarify accountability and responsibility.

> **NOTE**
>
> *Nurse managers must make every effort to turn a positive bottom line. Nurse managers who contribute positively to the organization's bottom line will not only remain gainfully employed, but will also contribute to the continued operation of the organization.*

The Integral Nature of Budgeting

People, not computers, make the budget work.

Budgeting is an integral part of the management of any organization. Specifically, budgeting is used in conjunction with the following:

- **Planning.** Budgeting is used in planning—that is, in assessing needs and setting future goals. There are two main forms of planning:

  - **Strategic planning.** This type of planning deals with how overall goals are to be met. It does not deal with future decisions, but rather with future implications of today's decisions. Poor financial decisions today will have a negative impact on strategic planning and goals in the future. Likewise, good financial decisions today can enable the organization to proceed with future plans, for example, new services.

> *Budgeting can lead to numerous benefits, but none can be realized unless you have total commitment at all levels of management within the organization. One can achieve this commitment only by working as a team. Communication is essential to this process. Top management must be transparent in creating a culture of fiscal awareness, where information about expenses and revenues is shared.*

- **Tactical planning.** This type of planning involves a series of 1-year plans designed to assist the organization in achieving its strategic goals in a prudent and timely manner. Organizations generally develop strategic plans for a 3-year period. Strategy involves costs. These costs must be planned in advance for the organization to be able to meet financial commitments of the future.

- **Monitoring.** In this phase, which involves resource allocation, management identifies activities for realizing planning goals. For example, suppose that a nurse manager recognizes that staff nurses are spending a minimum of 2 hours in shift report. This contributes to a significant amount of overtime, which the organization cannot afford. The nurse manager might then decide to implement walking shift report at patient bedsides, which drastically reduces the amount of time spent at shift report. The result is that overtime decreases and the unit functions more efficiently.

- **Controlling.** Significant variances should trigger further analysis and corrective action. This requires timely reporting and action. Nurse managers need to get comfortable with variance analysis at the time that budget reports are received and reviewed. This is done so that corrective action can take place prior to the next budget cycle. In other words, when negative budget variances exist (that is, when expenses exceed revenues), nurse managers must be able to determine the contributing factors. Usually, increased patient volume, inefficiency at the unit level (for example, the unit was overstaffed for volume), and the cost of staffing (for example, overtime was utilized too much) are what create the vast majority of variances.

Summary

This chapter covered the following:

- For-profit versus nonprofit healthcare organizations
- What a budget is
- The benefits of budgeting
- The integral nature of budgeting

References

Congressional Budget Office (CBO). (2006). *Nonprofit hospitals and the provision of community benefits.* Washington, DC: The Congress of the United States. Retrieved from https://www.cbo.gov/publication/18256?index=7695

Free Management Library. (n.d.). Retrieved from http://managementhelp.org/organizations/types.htm

2

Healthcare Reimbursement

To effectively budget, nurse managers must understand where healthcare dollars come from. Normally, when you purchase something—whether it's food at the grocery store, a new pair of shoes, or a car—you provide payment for that item at the time of purchase. With healthcare, however, things work a bit differently. Typically, when someone receives healthcare services, payment for those services is rendered later, either by the person's insurance company, government health programs, or out of the patient's pocket. This is known as *reimbursement*. A healthcare facility's reimbursements represent the bulk of its revenue.

This chapter provides an overview of political factors, historical and current, that affect healthcare policies and processes in the United States, including reimbursement. The chapter then outlines the history of healthcare reimbursement in the United States, covering per diem reimbursement, Medicare and Medicaid, managed care reimbursement, health maintenance organizations, preferred provider organizations, and accountable-care organizations.

It is important for nurses to understand both the political context and the history of healthcare reimbursement in the United States. While a vast majority of countries in Europe have a single-payer system, the United States is much different. The United States has an entrepreneurial healthcare system. It is market driven. Besides the federal government, each state is more or less like its own country. Legislation at both the federal and respective state level has shaped healthcare reimbursement in the United States. Gaining an understanding of where and when healthcare reimbursement began is critical to understanding where healthcare is today and, more importantly, where it is going in the future.

U.S. Healthcare: A Political Primer

Healthcare policy and financing are intricately intertwined. For example, in most Western countries, healthcare is a politically won universal right, with the government being the major guarantor of reimbursement. In the United States, however, the political consensus has traditionally favored a market-based approach to healthcare financing, with the individual being responsible to pay for care (either personally or through third-party arrangements with employer-provided healthcare plans or directly with insurers).

Public sentiment and political will in the United States have resulted in a diversion from a pure market-based approach when it comes to vulnerable populations and healthcare reimbursement. The elderly and disabled are covered by federal funds allocated to Medicare. Low-income persons are covered by a mix of federal and state funds allocated to Medicaid. Both Medicaid and Medicare are discussed later in this chapter.

Healthcare also carries with it political/social costs. These costs include the loss of individual income, the cost of medical care itself, and the cost of illness to society such as income interruption and decreased productivity. Social costs are also associated with lack of access to healthcare, such as poorer health and shorter life expectancy.

To better understand healthcare reimbursement, you want to know the general political history of healthcare in the United States. This section reviews that history from about 1929 to the current day.

This information about healthcare reimbursement in the United States is to provide you with an overview of how insurance plans began to develop. The early formation of such plans has provided a foundation for the type of healthcare delivery system and financing that exist today which is why it is useful to trace the history of this.

1929 to 1940

Before World War II, there were partially funded delivery systems of care. For example, when Blue Cross was initiated, only inpatient hospital care was funded. Outpatient care, such as a physician office visit and prescription medication, was not funded. Some employers provided onsite medical care for workers, with the rationale that worker productivity would thus be secure. This setup was not considered an employee benefit. Issues that affected healthcare policy, delivery, and cost prior to World War II included the growth and expansion of science and technology and developments in trauma care. In addition, infectious diseases were still prevalent because antibiotics were in their infancy.

In Europe, the move toward "socialized" medicine, or universal coverage via compulsory and nationalized health insurance, started before World War I. By the late 1930s, nearly every Western and Central European country had government-sponsored healthcare for employees and the disadvantaged. The United States did not follow this trend, however.

One major turning point in the American healthcare system occurred in 1929. That year was the beginning of the Great Depression. The Great Depression accelerated the privatization of healthcare coverage in the United States, originally as prepaid single-hospital service plans. Within 10 years, prepaid-premium plans with the Blue Cross designation were replicated in every state. Legislatures, physician groups, and healthcare institutions supported these plans. As a means of survival as finances became unstable, hospitals increasingly started accepting reimbursement from insurance companies. Because Blue Cross was the predominant insurer nationwide, hospitals began to seek their certification as a way to attract patients whose bills would certainly be paid. To attain Blue Cross designation, hospitals agreed to reduce price competition and to allow subscribers free choice of hospital and provider (thus severely undermining the single-hospital prepaid plans).

The 1930s are considered the development era of healthcare financing. During this period, healthcare policy and funding continued to change. Parallel development of prepaid group practices occurred. The popularity of prepaid medical care plans increased. Some healthcare providers balked at these changes, though. Even legislative action was invoked against consumer-run medical plans.

Blue Shield plans were developed during this period. These plans provided reimbursement specifically for physician services. The impetus for Blue Shield plans was physicians' fear of losing their practice autonomy (including diagnoses, schedule of care, and most importantly, their own fees) and the sanctity of the physician-patient relationship, based on the belief that insurance-accepting hospitals might start covering physician services under such plans.

1941 to 1964

As the United States entered World War II in 1941, more and more employers began to offer health insurance as an incentive/benefit to recruit and retain staff. The insurance plans benefited because these employee groups were less likely to be ill than older individuals not in the employment sector. Administrative costs were low because it was the working well who were enrolled in the plans. Most of the insured were covered by Blue Cross companies.

> **NOTE**
>
> *Employer-sponsored group healthcare programs began to proliferate during the 1940s. One reason that employers increasingly offered these plans was that U.S. government-mandated wage freezes during the war years meant that employers could not offer higher wages as a way to attract and retain workers. So instead, they began to offer group healthcare programs as part of their benefits packages.*

Post–World War II aspects of healthcare included a higher quality of life and increasing life expectancy. Labor unions had a major impact on healthcare coverage during this period. In 1948, the Supreme Court held that health insurance fell within the "conditions of employment" and was thus within the purview of union negotiation and collective bargaining (Inland Steel Co., n.d.). The unions paid a lot of attention to healthcare plans and fostered the development of employer-sponsored (or direct service) plans.

Unrestricted access to healthcare created cost inflation. In the 1950s, more than 60% of the population had hospital insurance. Employers generally paid more than 35% of healthcare premiums for their employees and more than 20% for employee dependents. The country lacked a national healthcare policy. There was resistance to restrictions on any part of the healthcare delivery system. Blue Cross at this time guaranteed full payment for services rendered, especially if the patient was treated in an inpatient hospital setting.

1965

The year 1965 was a pivotal year for healthcare. Lyndon Baines Johnson, then President of the United States, implemented what former President John F. Kennedy had been working on: Medicare and Medicaid. These were considered new social programs. Medicare was targeted to insure the elderly and special populations such as dialysis patients. Medicaid was targeted to cover the working poor. The implementation of Medicare and Medicaid represented an expanded role of government in the financing and organizing of the healthcare delivery system in the United States.

1980s

The 1980s saw a proliferation of health maintenance organizations (HMOs) and prepaid group plans. Such plans and HMOs provided cost controls during this time by maintaining their own hospitals and clinics or by making payment arrangements with specific hospitals and providers. They also employed their own physician staff and other staff members. HMOs removed the fee-for-service incentive from providers. They also kept rates of utilization low.

HMOs also have lower rates of utilization of advanced medical technology.

The Debate Over National Health Insurance

Let's diverge now from our timeline review of healthcare policy changes in the United States and talk about the debate that has influenced healthcare policy at many points in the past, has stalled at other times, and has recently become a topic that initiates lively discussion at political rallies (to say nothing of family get-togethers): national health insurance.

National health insurance has been debated in the United States for decades. The principle dates back to the 1930s, but at that time, President Franklin D. Roosevelt favored passage of the Social Security Bill of 1935; he feared that including a compulsory national health insurance component to that bill or as a separate piece of legislation might doom passage of Social Security. In 1943, the Wagner-Murray-Dingell Bill was introduced in Congress. This piece of legislation proposed a national health plan to insure every American citizen. The bill was defeated in 1950 after fierce opposition by the American Medical Association (AMA). The AMA's position was to oppose a bill that would result in what they believed would be the enslavement of the medical profession.

A resurgence of public discussion about a national healthcare plan occurred in the 1950s and in the 1960s. In the 1980s, Senator Edward Kennedy of Massachusetts kept the issue of a national healthcare plan in the headlines. In the 1990s, a discussion about a national healthcare plan again dominated headlines. This latter discussion occurred under President Bill Clinton's administration, in the first hundred days of his presidency, when he appointed his wife Hillary Rodham Clinton to develop a national health plan. This bill was also defeated.

Finally though, in 2010, Congress passed the Patient Protection and Affordable Care Act (ACA), which President Barack Obama then signed into law. The ACA seeks to insure those American citizens who before the act were either uninsurable (because of a preexisting condition, for instance) or uninsured (usually because they could not afford the premiums because of their lower economic status).

2003

The Medicare Prescription Drug, Improvement, and Modernization Act of 2003 (a.k.a. Medicare Modernization Act of 2003 or MMA) amends Title XVIII of the Social Security Act to provide for a voluntary prescription drug benefit under the Medicare program and to strengthen and improve the Medicare program, and for other purposes.

Under the MMA initial physical exams and referral for screening and other preventive services were covered under Medicare beginning in January 2005.

Cardiovascular screening blood tests were permitted, which include cholesterol, other lipids, and triglyceride serum levels. Diabetes screening tests were also added for coverage, including fasting plasma glucose tests and other tests appropriate for persons at high risk for diabetes.

This act made Medicare prescription drug plans available beginning in January 2006. These plans were offered through private prescription drug plans (PDPs). The drug plan also can be offered by Medicare Advantage Plans. To be eligible and enroll in the plan, an individual had to be entitled to Part A of Medicare and enrolled in Part B of Medicare. Enrollment was voluntary. There were increased premiums for those people who waited to enroll that included 1% of the base premium for each month the individual did not enroll. An exception was placed in the act for those who were covered under other comparable insurance.

Why would an individual want to join the prescription drug plan? Medical practices incorporate new drug therapies to treat chronic conditions, and this practice is increasing. Out-of-pocket spending on drugs has increased. As people age, it is more likely they will need prescription drugs to remain healthy.

Medicare insurance coverage for prescription drugs was designed to protect individuals from high out-of-pocket costs. This plan is available for all people with Medicare and is provided through PDPs, Medicare health plans, and some employers and unions for retirees.

When the plan was initiated, individuals would pay a premium of about $37 each month in addition to the Part B premium. An enhanced benefit could cost more. There was a yearly deductible up to $250. And the plan paid part of the cost of covered prescription drugs.

However, there was a doughnut hole in the plan. An individual would pay 100% of cost after a certain limit of payment was reached by the Medicare Part D prescription plan. Individuals with limited resources could get extra help with their Medicare drug plan costs. For the lowest income levels, individuals did not have to pay premiums or deductibles, or they paid small or no copayments.

Persons with Medicare have to reside in the United States. They must meet the income and resource requirements of the subsidy program, and they have to be enrolled in Medicare. The doughnut hole will be closed by 2020 through provisions outlined in the ACA.

What is a Medicare Advantage Plan? This is an alternative way to get Medicare benefits. The term Medicare Advantage Plans replaced the term Medicare + Choice plans. Such plans were generally offered by preferred provider organizations (PPOs).

Private fee-for-service plans were also available in some states. Medicare specialty plans were also available. Those who joined a Medicare Advantage Plan still have the same rights and protections under the Medicare program. They still get all regular Medicare-covered services. In addition, they may be eligible for extra benefits such as coverage for extra days in a hospital.

Patients with Medicare have rights. They have the right to information about all treatment choices, to participate in treatment decisions, to get easy-to-understand information, and to know what costs are paid by Medicare and which costs they have to pay.

Participants in the Medicare plans also have the right to receive emergency department services, to have their personal health information kept secure and private, and the right to nondiscrimination. A patient cannot be treated unfairly because of race, color, national origin, disability, age, gender, or religion.

Patients with Medicare also have the right to know what to do if they have to file an appeal or grievance. Such appeals can be filed when Medicare does not make payment, when Medicare does not pay enough, or when the patient is not provided with the service covered under Medicare. Generally a grievance is about quality-of-care issues.

> **NOTE**
>
> *It should also be noted that patients with Alzheimer's disease enrolled in the Medicare program have the same rights and coverage that any other person has with Medicare.*

2010

The driving forces of healthcare delivery today are access, quality, and cost control. Generally, when a new business is started, the cost line increases as well as the quality line. After the business is operational for a while, the quality line usually increases, and the cost line levels off or lowers.

In healthcare, the opposite has traditionally occurred in the United States. The cost line continues to rise, and the quality line lowers, which is the complete opposite of what should happen.

The increased cost in the U.S. healthcare delivery system stems from higher administrative fees and the increasing cost of technology and pharmaceuticals; these two factors alone result in U.S. healthcare expenses far exceeding those of other nations.

As mentioned in the preceding section, the ACA seeks to insure American citizens who before the act were either uninsurable or uninsured. As you'll learn in the more detailed discussion about the ACA in Chapter 9, the act also addresses quality and cost. The Institute of Medicine (IOM) has also been a major player in trying to improve quality in the U.S. healthcare delivery system.

Also included in the ACA is the concept of accountable care organizations (ACOs). The ACO consists of a medical home, which is usually primary care or a clinic. The purpose of the medical home is disease management, with an oversight of patients wherever they are in the healthcare delivery system.

Bundled billing and payment is a critical aspect of an ACO. Quality of care and costs are managed judiciously. Increased payment is received if the quality of care is excellent. Value-based purchasing is a critical component of this concept. The key questions in an ACO are:

- What value is assured to the patient?

- What value is the patient receiving by purchasing a certain organization's healthcare services?

For example, one hospital has one guaranteed price regardless of outcome. Should a patient have open heart surgery and postoperatively that patient develops a surgical wound infection requiring readmission, there is no additional charge to the patient or the insurance company because there was a guaranteed fixed price for quality.

In such an organization, if quality problems continue to occur, payment is reduced to the provider, which creates an incentive for them to improve quality so that they will be paid more.

ACOs are demonstrating significant cost savings with improved quality of care to the patient. Quality must exist throughout any service offered in an ACO.

Home care is a critical component of an ACO. Insurance companies will pay for home care services because generally these services are less costly than hospital admissions and can even prevent hospital admissions and readmissions.

NOTE

For a more detailed discussion about home care, see Chapter 11.

Healthcare Reimbursement in the United States: How Things Used to Be

In the 1970s, reimbursement was most often based on a per diem rate, paid by insurers. A *per diem rate* is a daily fee or rate that is billed and paid. Thus, hospitals were simply reimbursed whatever they charged. In the 1970s, the payer was typically Blue Cross and Blue Shield, as well as Medicare and Medicaid.

Hospitals would charge a per diem rate or daily rate for hospital services. Such rates were generally calculated by averaging daily expenses incurred over the entire hospital census. Such rates were usually reviewed and approved by hospital rate setting commissions in each respective state. Such state commissions would be established through the state's legislative process.

The other form of reimbursement during this period was self-pay reimbursement. That is, a patient would pay what was billed. For example, in 1970, when my first child was born, he had a congenital hernia that needed repair. Because at that time I did not have a job that provided health insurance, I set up a payment plan with the hospital, to which I made a monthly payment until the bill was paid in full.

Under both these systems, hospitals had no incentive to discharge patients early, because hospitals basically were paid what they billed. By the latter part of the 1970s, however, insurance providers began to question the generous reimbursements to hospitals. In an effort to control healthcare costs, these companies introduced the Diagnosis Related Group (DRG) system. This was a system of averages; rather than paying a daily rate, insurance companies using the DRG system paid a case rate. Under this system, which was adopted nationally under Medicare, insurance companies began to control healthcare costs. For the first time, hospitals had an incentive to discharge patients early.

NOTE

With any system, there is usually a way around it. This was true for the DRG system. Providers learned their way around the DRG maze to maximize reimbursements. For example, the key person in maximizing revenue under the DRG system was the DRG coder in medical records. This person reviewed the medical record in detail. Once coded correctly, certain terminology used in the medical record could lead to increased case rates of reimbursement.

Third-party payers also began negotiating for discount rates. The difference between the amount charged and the amount paid under these discount rates was known as the *contractual allowance.*

The Early Role of Insurance Companies

Insurance companies were originally devised to cover acute care hospitalization. Initially, the primary insurance company was Blue Cross and Blue Shield. Going back to the 1970s, this insurance product covered services for inpatient hospitalization far more than outpatient services. For example, a typical plan (from my own experience) might cover $25 for outpatient care for an entire family for a 1-year time period. However, if the patient was admitted to the hospital, all procedures were covered.

> **NOTE**
>
> *Patients were often admitted to acute care hospitals for testing procedures even though such procedures could be completed in an outpatient setting. That was because patients would have been responsible for most of the charges had the procedures been performed on an outpatient basis.*

The Advent of Medicare and Medicaid

As noted earlier in the chapter, to provide insurance for the elderly and other poor/vulnerable populations, Medicare and Medicaid were implemented by the U.S. government in 1965 under President Lyndon B. Johnson.

Medicare consists of four parts:

- **Part A.** This covers inpatient care in hospitals, skilled nursing facilities, and hospice care, and provides care for specific patient populations (for example, dialysis patients). Medicare Part A covers the first 20 days in a skilled nursing facility if the patient was previously admitted to an acute care hospital for a minimum of 3 nights, had a valid diagnosis, and was transferred from the acute care hospital to the skilled nursing facility. After the 20 days in the skilled nursing facility, Medicare Part A covers the next 80 days in the nursing home at 80%.

- **Part B.** This covers outpatient care, such as physician office visits, durable medical equipment, physical therapy, and other services.

- **Part C.** This is a Medicare Advantage Plan, much like an HMO or a PPO, which are discussed later in the chapter. This is a health plan choice that a person may have as part of Medicare. Medicare advantage plans, sometimes called *Part C* or *MA plans*, are offered by private companies approved by Medicare.

- **Part D.** This is the prescription drug plan, enacted in 2005 under President George W. Bush. This plan covers up to $2,700 per year. After that amount has been spent, the patient falls into the "doughnut hole," meaning that he or she is responsible for the next $4,350 of expenditures. After that, the plan picks up again and continues to cover costs. As previously noted, one of the provisions of the ACA is to close the doughnut hole over a course of years. Note that for a person to get Medicare prescription drug coverage, he or she must join a plan run by an insurance company or other private company approved by Medicare. Each plan varies in terms of cost and drugs covered.

The parts that affect healthcare reimbursement the greatest are Parts A, B, and D.

As mentioned, Medicaid was also enacted at this time. This program was designed for the poor. Both the federal government and state governments fund this program.

The administrative department of the federal government that oversees these programs is known as the Centers for Medicare & Medicaid Services (CMS).

The Role of Philanthropy

When an individual or an organization donates money to a healthcare facility such as a hospital, that donation constitutes philanthropy in healthcare reimbursements. Philanthropic donations can assist organizations in providing care. Many philanthropic organizations donate large sums of money, often in exchange for the hospital naming a wing of the facility after the donor.

Managed Care

As healthcare costs increased, insurance companies ushered in managed care in the early 1990s. *Managed care* refers to any system that manages healthcare delivery with the goal of controlling costs.

Managed care systems typically incorporate a primary care base. Primary care functions as a gatekeeper through whom the patient has to go to obtain other health services, such as specialty medical care, surgery, or physical therapy.

The managed care model has definitely controlled costs through the control of procedures and hospital admissions. Some of the key elements of managed care include the following:

- Selective contracting

- Price competition

- Creation of integrated health networks

- Emergence of large physician groups

- Dominance of insurance companies

- Geographic growth of for-profit institutions

The outcomes in managed care are achieved through decreased lengths of hospital stays, denial of certain procedures, case management and critical pathways, minimally invasive procedures, the bundling of services and payment, capitation, and a focus on patient outcomes, both from a physical standpoint and a quality of care standpoint.

WHY THE RISING COSTS?

Healthcare costs rise for many reasons. One reason is an increase in labor costs. Another reason is that advances in technology bring new types of care that involve increased costs. In addition, pharmaceutical costs continue to rise, as do malpractice insurance premiums for providers.

Today, there are the following main kinds of managed care products:

- **Health maintenance organizations (HMOs):** The purpose of this first type of managed care product was (and is) to focus on health promotion and prevention of illness. Primary care, women's health services, and other such services are generally reimbursed under HMOs. When participating in an HMO, patients must select a primary care provider; the primary care provider then makes referrals as needed to specialists.

- **Preferred provider organizations (PPOs):** A preferred provider organization, sometimes referred to as a *participating provider organization*, is essentially a managed care organization of medical doctors, hospitals, and other healthcare providers who have covenanted with an insurer or a third-party administrator to provide healthcare at reduced rates to the insurer's or administrator's clients. In a PPO, patients are referred by the insurance company to preferred providers, with whom the company has a contract.

- **Point of service plans (POSs):** This type of managed care plan has characteristics of both an HMO and a PPO, and offers more flexibility. In a POS plan, the patient selects a primary care provider from a list of participating providers. All medical care is directed by this provider; the provider is the patient's "point of service." Referrals are made to other in-network providers should a specialist be needed. There is a broad base of medical providers in the POS network, which typically covers a large geographic area.

- **Independent provider associations (IPAs):** Some physicians may form an IPA within a particular specialty or primary care workgroup. An independent provider association, also referred to as an independent practice association, is an association of independent physicians or other organizations that contracts with independent physicians. Services are provided to managed care organizations on a negotiated per capita rate, flat retainer fee, or negotiated fee-for-service basis. An HMO or other managed care plan may contract with an IPA, which in turn contracts with independent physicians to treat members at discounted fees or on a capitation basis.

Types of Healthcare Reimbursement

Table 2.1 summarizes the previous discussion and lists the various types of reimbursement in the United States for the provision of healthcare.

TABLE 2.1

METHODS OF REIMBURSEMENT

Types of Reimbursement	Explanation
Per diem rate	Pay billable daily rate.
Medicare	Federal system of reimbursement enacted in 1965 by President Lyndon B. Johnson. Medicare has four parts: A (acute care hospitalization and nursing home reimbursement); B (outpatient care, for example, physical therapy; primary care office visits); C (Medicare Advantage Plans); and D (prescription plan). Medicare pays a fixed amount per inpatient, based on the discharge diagnosis.
Medicaid	Title XIX enacted in 1965 by President Lyndon B. Johnson. Medicaid provides insurance for the poor. The federal government and states share in costs. Medicaid usually pays less than stated charges, varying the amount from state to state.
Managed care	Effort by insurance companies to control costs and balance quality.
HMO	Short for health maintenance organization. The focus of HMOs is on primary care and prevention.
PPO	Short for preferred provider organization. With a PPO, the insurance company contracts with certain providers.

Types of Reimbursement	Explanation
IPA	Short for independent provider (or practice) association. An association of independent physicians or other organizations that contracts with independent physicians. Services are provided to managed care organizations.
Self-pay	In this model, the individual pays for care.
Philanthropy	In this model, funds are received from donors. Free or charity care is provided by most institutions to some degree. Some states have a charity care pool or fund; these funds tend to reimburse those hospitals that offer the most charity care. Often, community hospitals receive little or no payment for charity care.

NOTE

Some donors who make financial contributions place restrictions on their use. These are called restricted resources. With restricted resources, the donor earmarks the area in which the donation should be applied (hospice, cardiac care, pediatric facilities, and so on).

Of course, sometimes no payment is made. The fact is, many Americans are uninsured. And given the late 2000s recession and general economic climate, even those who *are* insured may not be able to afford their copays.

This situation means that some patients simply cannot pay their bills. In other cases, insurance companies deny payments to healthcare facilities. They might claim that care given was not medically necessary or that a patient's continued stay was not medically required, or they might blame the healthcare facility for an iatrogenic event (a medical problem resulting from the fault of the provider) that resulted in the patient staying longer. All this is to say that in some cases, facilities might not be compensated for care given. Income lost because of failure of patients or contractors to pay owed amounts is called *bad debt*.

Capitation

Another form of healthcare reimbursement is capitation. In its simplest form, *capitation* is a set reimbursement methodology that is applied regardless of how many times a patient accesses a provider. For example, with capitation, which evolved during the 1990s, an insurance company might reimburse a primary care provider $10 per month, regardless of whether a patient sees the provider once per month, five times per month, or not at all.

There are six basic types of capitation:

- **Partnership capitation:** In this model, the physician and the hospital to which the physician refers patients work collaboratively. The goal is cost-effective care, both in the provider's office and at the hospital (if a patient requires hospitalization).

- **Network capitation:** An example of this type of capitation would be a healthcare organization that owns multiple acute care hospitals. All these hospitals would be in a capitated model with a particular insurance plan.

- **System capitation:** An example of this type of capitation would be a hospital system that owns more than just acute care hospitals. For example, the hospital system might own several acute care hospitals, long-term care facilities, assisted-living facilities, and offer access to pharmaceuticals, durable medical equipment, outpatient physical therapy, and home care. A patient in a capitated plan would be capitated across the system.

- **Chronic disease capitation:** An example of this type of capitation would be the capitation of care for certain chronic illnesses, such as diabetes, HIV infection, heart failure, and other such illnesses. In other words, rather than an insurance company reimbursing every diagnosis, only certain chronic illness diagnoses would be capitated.

- **Carve-out capitation:** An example of carve-out capitation would be an insurance company that carves out certain diagnoses that are not chronic in nature and capitates them—for example, cataract surgery, total joint surgery, and other such nonchronic illnesses.

- **Medicare capitation:** An example of this type of capitation would be the Medicare program reimbursing acute care hospitals under a capitated model rather than the DRG system.

To summarize, Table 2.2 lists the various types of capitation.

If you were to compare proposed insurance models, capitation would save the most money. In a capitated model, risks for patient care are shared both by the provider and the insurance carrier, with the vast majority of risk being taken by the provider.

TABLE 2.2
TYPES OF CAPITATED CARE MODELS

Types of Capitation	Explanation
Partnership capitation	The primary care office and hospital work collaboratively in a capitated model of payment.
Network capitation	A hospital owns multiple acute-care hospitals, all of which are capitated in an insurance product.
System capitation	A hospital system is in a capitated model in an insurance plan across services (that is, acute care, long-term care, outpatient care, home care).
Chronic disease capitation	Certain chronic illnesses are reimbursed in a capitated model (for example, HIV, diabetes mellitus, heart failure).
Carve-out capitation	Certain illnesses other than chronic diseases are in a capitated model (for example, total joint replacement surgical procedures, cataract with IOL implant procedures).
Medicare capitation	Medicare reimburses acute care hospitals in a capitated model of payment rather than the DRG form of payment.

TURNING A POSITIVE FINANCIAL LINE

In recent years, managed care and federal, state, and other insurance programs have significantly reduced reimbursement to hospitals and providers. Therefore, it is very challenging for most hospitals and providers to turn a positive financial line on operations. Think about it: If a hospital has a 2% positive line on operations on, say, a $100,000,000 budget, the hospital has turned a profit of $2,000,000. That might sound like a lot of money, but in today's world, it is not. In most hospitals, one bad month could result in the loss of that $2,000,000 profit.

The Role of Social Policy

When I was a vice president for nursing in a hospital, the director of education at the same facility was on the board of the New Jersey State Nurses Association Political Action Committee (PAC). One year, a federal bill was sponsored that would drastically reduce Medicare payments to acute care hospitals.

In response, the director of education, also a nurse, mounted tables outside our hospital's cafeteria and staffed them with volunteers. Anytime an employee visited the cafeteria, a volunteer at the table asked them to read a summary of the proposed legislation and to sign a petition urging our congressional representative to vote against the legislation. Then, another volunteer at the table dialed the congressional representative's office, handed the phone to the employee, and advised the employee to tell the congressional representative's aide to tell the congressman to vote against the legislation.

Within a few days, this congressman had received more than 1,000 pieces of mail and more than 1,000 telephone calls on this issue. Fortunately, he heard the message. Our congressional representative was one of four Republicans who voted against this Republican-sponsored legislation.

(Incidentally, this congressional representative is still in office, and has been reelected several times. Why? Because he listens to his constituents and addresses their concerns.)

All this is to say that nurses responsible for budgeting in their organizations must have a general understanding of social policy both at the federal and state levels. Why? Because healthcare dollars and social policy are intertwined. For example, suppose that the federal government changes reimbursement policies in the Medicare system such that there is less reimbursement for patient care providers. This could translate to layoffs of personnel in a hospital or other provider setting. As another example, this one at the state level, consider New Jersey, where charity care is funded by the state. If the state's social policy were to reduce charity care funding, each hospital providing such charity care would experience a decrease in reimbursement.

NURSES AS POLITICAL ACTIVISTS

Nurses must be politically active when proposed legislation is moving through the system. Nurses can become politically active in various ways:

- **Become a registered voter:** Congressional representatives, senators, and other political figures will not listen to anyone who is not a registered voter. Votes are what put and keep political figures in office.

- **Participate in grassroots efforts:** A simple way to become politically involved is through grassroots efforts (for example, writing or calling members of Congress and advising them how they should vote on a healthcare issue and why).

- **Lobby:** National and state nursing organizations have lobbyists. Many of these organizations also have political action committees that survey individuals running for office. They assess candidates' political platforms and endorse for their membership the political candidates they believe best represent their position.

- **Run for office:** Some nurses run for political office themselves, such as for a seat on the city council or for mayor or for the state legislature.

The bottom line? It is important to be in tune with legislation that affects not only our practice as nurses but also reimbursement for healthcare services.

Accountable Care Organizations

One of the most significant social policy initiatives at the federal government level is accountable care organizations (ACOs). Various healthcare systems are currently exploring ACO models. The purpose of an ACO is to reduce costs and improve quality of healthcare.

Currently, reimbursement occurs in silos, with separate bills for acute care, rehab, home care, and so on. For example, suppose a patient receives a total hip replacement. That patient is initially seen in primary care. When a diagnosis is made, the patient is referred to an orthopedic specialist, who recommends a total hip replacement. The hip replacement is performed in the acute care setting, after which the patient is transferred to a rehab facility, and then sent home, where the patient receives physical therapy. The patient then receives separate bills from each of these settings. Figure 2.1 illustrates this model.

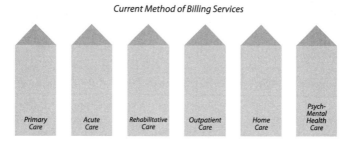

Current Method of Billing Services

Each Type of Service Bills Independent of the Other Services

FIGURE 2.1
The current reimbursement model.

In contrast, with an ACO, one bill covers all these settings (see Figure 2.2). If one of the settings were to render poor-quality care, thus increasing the patient's length of stay, all these settings would suffer the consequences. Therefore, there is pressure on the provider rendering the poorer quality care to improve; otherwise, the other two providers could elect to partner with another provider that provides better quality.

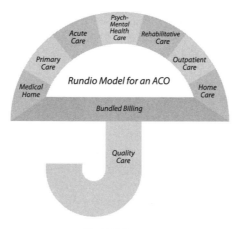

FIGURE 2.2
The ACO reimbursement model.

In some ACO models, physicians become employees of the ACO, and their reimbursement level is correlated with the quality of care provided. The better the quality, the better the reimbursement to the provider.

The Importance of Reimbursement: An Example

Budgeting in a hospital setting isn't so different from managing your personal checking and savings accounts. Take me as an example. I receive revenue for the work that I do:

- I receive a salary for my full-time job as a clinical professor of nursing and as the department chair.

- I receive money for offering consulting services to nursing organizations.

- I receive payment to practice part-time.

On the other side of the coin, I have expenses. Specifically, I have to pay for my mortgage, car, electricity, food, clothing, and daily travel expenses (and other related expenses). If my expenses are greater than my income, I cannot pay all my bills. In other words, my expenses cannot exceed my income.

All this is to say that I have money coming in and money going out, on a daily, weekly, biweekly, monthly, and annual basis. The same holds true for a hospital or healthcare system. If the hospital's reimbursements are lower than its expenditures, the hospital could go bankrupt. To break even, expenses will have to be reduced.

Managers need to know how to manipulate variables to produce the greatest cost benefit for their unit. Examples of such variables include staffing, staff mix, supplies, overtime, allocation of productive and nonproductive time, and other variables. This is not magic; it is a matter of utilizing resources. Money comes in, and money goes out.

PROBLEMS FACING THE HEALTHCARE DELIVERY SYSTEM

Today, the healthcare delivery system in the United States faces three major problems:

- **Access to care:** There are approximately 57 million Americans with no healthcare insurance, and this estimate may be low given the high unemployment rates of the late 2000s (The Henry J. Kaiser Foundation, 2015). These individuals lack access to the system in the literal sense.

- **Quality:** Although the United States has some of the best technology available, our outcomes pale in comparison to other nations' outcomes. Our healthcare delivery system focuses on intervention rather than prevention. Costly and invasive procedures and tests do not translate into improved outcomes.

- **Cost:** The United States has one of the most costly healthcare delivery systems. Due to decreasing revenue streams resulting from controlled and decreased reimbursement rates by managed care and from the federal government and state governments, it is becoming more and more difficult for healthcare organizations to make a profit, or even break even.

Summary

This chapter covered the following:

- An overview of healthcare reimbursement in the United States

- Political history of healthcare reimbursement in the United States

- The Medicare Prescription Drug, Improvement, and Modernization Act of 2003

- Per diem reimbursement

- Medicare (Parts A, B, C, and D)

- Medicaid

- Managed care reimbursement

- Health maintenance organizations

- Preferred provider organizations

- Independent provider (or practice) organizations

- Accountable care organizations

References

The Henry J. Kaiser Foundation. (2015). Key Facts about the Uninsured Population. Retrieved at http://kff.org/uninsured/fact-sheet/key-facts-about-the-uninsured-population

Inland Steel Co. (n.d.). [077 NLRB No. 001], Case no. 13-C-02836. National Labor Relations Board (NLRB). Retrieved from apps.nlrb.gov

3

Budget Types

When I was a new nurse manager, I had no clue that several types of budgets existed. I was truly budget naïve. Since then, through many years of management, I have learned that healthcare organizations use many types of budgets. These include the following:

- Master budgets
- Operating budgets
- Capital budgets
- Program budgets

Operating budgets and the capital budgets are further broken down into unit budgets, so nurse managers can effectively develop, monitor, and manage their own budgets. Operating and capital budgets are the two budgets that nurse managers construct and monitor most often; therefore, you'll learn much more about these types of budget throughout the rest of the book.

> **NOTE**
>
> *The vast majority of budgets are constructed for a 1-year time period.*

To begin our journey, let's start with some basic accounting principles.

Accrual Versus Cash Basis for Accounting

There are three major components to the budget process, as follows:

- Assets
- Liabilities
- Equity

Assets are resources that are owned usually stated as current assets, fixed assets, and noncurrent assets.

Examples of current assets include cash and other assets that can be converted to cash within a 1-year time period.

Liabilities are the opposite of assets. A liability is an obligation that needs to be paid. Current liabilities are obligations due to be paid within a 1-year time period. Examples include wages and taxes. Long-term liabilities are obligations or debts that are not due within a 1-year time period. Examples include a mortgage, a car loan or other loan, and a home-improvement loan.

Equity is associated with assets and liabilities. Equity is the excess of assets over liabilities. These are inclusive of resources invested by the owner. Some individuals refer to this as the fund balance or the net worth.

Equity can be increased or decreased. The way to increase equity is through investment by the owner and by profits of an organization. Many individuals invest in 401(k) plans in order to have equity when they retire. The way to decrease equity is through the withdrawal of assets or cash or if the there are losses from an unprofitable business.

$$\text{Assets} = \text{Liabilities} + \text{Equity}$$

$$\text{Equity} = \text{Assets} - \text{Liabilities}$$

For example, to purchase a $350,000 home, a buyer puts down savings of $70,000 and obtains a mortgage for $280,000.

Assets = $350,000 Liability = $280,000 Equity = $70,000

$$A = L + E$$

$$(\$350,000 = \$280,000 + \$70,000)$$

or

$$A - L = E$$

$$(\$350,000 - \$280,000 = \$70,000)$$

The cash budget is an estimation of future cash receipts and payment that are tabulated to display the forecasted cash balance.

The balance sheet represents the organization's assets minus liabilities plus equity at a point in time. Usually, the balance sheet is prepared at the end of a month or at the end of a year. Figure 3.1 shows an example balance sheet for a specialty nursing organization.

Revenue is the amount charged to customers for goods and services.

Expenses are costs that are incurred by a business.

The profit or net income is the amount of revenue that exceeds expenses.

Profit = Revenue – Expenses

Revenue and expenses are tracked over a specific period of time. This is known as the *accounting period*. A fiscal year would be a 12-month accounting period. The time that a fiscal year begins and ends depends the organization. The most common fiscal years are as follows:

- January 1 to December 31

- July 1 to June 30

- October 1 to September 30

Revenues and expenses are generally measured on either a cash basis or an accrual basis. A cash basis recognizes revenues when cash is received and when expenses are paid out. An accrual basis recognizes revenues when services are to be performed or goods are to be sold and expenses occur when the obligation is to be paid or the resource is to be utilized.

Accounts receivable are the dollars that the organization is expecting to be paid. Accounts receivable generally is anywhere from 60 to 90 days. The accrual basis of accounting tends to be a more accurate accounting measurement that most organizations subscribe to.

Businesses make revenue and have associated costs. The break-even point is when revenue exactly equals the sum of fixed and variable costs or total cost. Break-even then results when costs are exactly equal to revenues. The goal of any business is to have revenue exceed expenses.

CURRENT ASSETS		CURRENT LIABILITIES	
Bank Account	$70,000.00	Accounts Payable	$10,000.00
Money Market	$100,000.00	Deferred Revenue (Dues 2013-2014)	$30,000.00
Bank Interest	$7,000.00	Total Deferred Revenue	$30,000.00
TOTAL BANK FUNDS	**$177,000.00**	**TOTAL CURRENT LIABILITIES**	**$40,000.00**
ACCOUNTS RECEIVABLE	$14,000.00	**NET ASSETS**	
Property & Equipment	$22,000.00	Beginning Net Assets	$115,000.00
Accumulated Depreciation	$(11,000.00)	Restricted - Chapters	$10,000.00
		Revenues Over (Under) Expenses	$50,000.00
P&E NET	**$11,000.00**	**TOTAL NET ASSETS**	**$175,000.00**
Investments	$12,000.00		
Investments in & Advances to Affiliates	$1,000.00	**TOTAL LIABILITIES**	**$40,000.00**
TOTAL ASSETS	**$215,000.00**	**TOTAL LIABILITIES & NET ASSETS**	$215,000.00

FIGURE 3.1
Balance Sheet for Specialty Nursing Organization.

Responsibility Center Budgeting

Let's begin with a definition of direct and indirect costs.

- **Direct costs:** A price that can be completely attributed to the production of specific goods or services. Examples of direct costs are materials, labor, and expenses related to the production of a product.

- **Indirect costs:** Costs that are not directly associated with a single activity, event, or other object. Such costs are usually aggregated into an overhead cost pool and allocated to various activities, based on an allocation method that has a perceived or actual linkage between the indirect cost and the activity. Costs such as depreciation or administrative expenses are more difficult to assign to a specific product, and therefore are considered indirect costs.

Examples of indirect costs include the following:

- Management salaries and related benefits
- Quality assurance staff wages and related benefits
- Equipment maintenance
- Facility rent
- Utilities

Examples of administrative indirect costs include the following:

- Corporate salaries
- Depreciation on office equipment
- Facility rent
- Utilities

Under traditional approaches to budgeting, operating units often are held accountable for the management of direct costs. Examples of direct costs include salaries and wages, materials and supplies, travel, and equipment acquisition and maintenance. The assumption is that such direct costs can be controlled. The smaller the number of direct costs, the larger the amount of indirect costs.

Technically, all costs are controllable by someone within an organization. It is generally much easier to control direct costs compared to indirect costs. For example, I can control overtime and make certain that employees are being paid the total hours budgeted. It is more difficult to control items such as heating, ventilation and air conditioning, or the costs allocated to my department for the mortgage on the building.

Under responsibility center budgeting, all pertinent costs and the revenue to support these costs are assigned to various organizational units that are designated as responsibility centers. Responsibility center budgeting seeks to assign accountability to those individuals who have the greatest potential to exercise influence, on a day-to-day basis, over the costs. In nursing this individual is usually the nurse manager for the respective nursing unit; however, this may vary from organization to organization.

It is the reporting responsibility of these individuals to explain the outcome regardless of the degree of their control or influence over the results. The vice president of nursing might receive separate reports on the cost of operations for the medical surgical nursing units, the critical care units, the emergency department, and the operating room. Each individual unit will be held accountable for its respective area of responsibility.

Costs charged to the responsibility centers need to be distinguished between direct and indirect costs. Not every indirect cost is controllable at the responsibility center level. These expenses need to be further broken down between those that are controllable and those that are not controllable.

Responsibility center budgeting places emphasis on specific costs in relation to well-defined areas of responsibility. Responsibility management centers may be able to exercise considerable control over such traditional indirect costs as utilities and building maintenance, but such costs as depreciation, long-term lease arrangements, and other similar costs rarely qualify as controllable costs.

Responsibility centers have primary responsibility for the management of resources and costs (as well as the broader mission for which these resources and costs are budgeted and allocated). All the sources of financial support (revenue or income) are attributed to the responsibility centers on some equitable and consistent basis. Costs associated with internal service units (that is, units which do not receive revenue or income from external sources) are either charged to the responsibility centers on a fee for service basis or are recovered from the responsibility centers through some form of assessment. An example of an internal service unit would be the environmental services department or the security department in a hospital.

Once income/revenue and costs have been fully allocated to the responsibility centers, in all likelihood there will be some "surpluses" and some "deficits." When budgets are prepared well, the revenue should equal costs or ideally revenue should exceed the costs. The reality is that this is a very difficult thing to accomplish. Rarely does revenue equal costs. The goal is to produce a surplus, but at times budget expenses exceed revenue, creating a deficit.

Deficits or shortfalls between total costs and revenues/income must be covered through some form of subvention. Subvention is a central allocation to ensure the continued operation of programs existing at the time the new allocation model is implemented. Some organizations create a subvention tax for each responsibility center. The purpose of the tax is to make "whole" those responsibility centers that have a deficit shortfall. One of the newer terms being touted for subvention tax is a participation tax. All responsibility centers participate in this tax, again, for the purpose of making all centers whole. Responsibility centers should be permitted to retain all or a major portion of their surpluses as this creates incentive to have revenue and income exceed expenses.

What is the source of the funds used for the subvention or participation tax? One approach is to "take funds off the top"(that is, to hold back some portion of the general funds to cover these costs). Another approach is to initiate a surcharge or "assessment" on the expenditure of the resources that have been fully allocated. The revenue collected through this levy could then be reallocated to the responsibility centers, both as subvention to provide a level playing field for those units faced with deficits and to "seed" additional activities that may have organization-wide benefits. A portion of the assessment could also be used to support internal service units.

Responsibility center budgeting with use of a subvention or participation tax is utilized most in universities (in particular, research-intensive universities), as a portion of the subvention or participation tax from each school or college within the university is utilized to fund research activities across the university.

Various Forms of Budgets

Master budgets, operating budgets, capital budgets, and program budgets can take various forms. These include the following:

- Zero-based budgets
- Fixed budgets
- Flexible budgets

The form used for a budget depends on the organization's philosophy. If the organization is fiscally conservative, a fixed budget is typically used. Some organizations are more flexible, in which case flexible budgeting may be utilized, where information in the budget is updated quarterly rather than remaining static for a year. Zero-based budgets are performed periodically as a check and balance on a historical budget or when a major paradigm shift in healthcare reimbursement has occurred.

Most institutions also generate a historical budget, which includes prior historical data on operations. This historical budget is used in the creation of the various fiscal budgets.

Zero-Based Budgets

A zero-based budget begins as a *tabula rasa*, or blank slate. Zero-based budgets are completed for brand new services or organizations. In a zero-based budget, there is no prior history. The organization's finance department would have to estimate revenue and expenses based on an assessment of the community, national trends, market penetration of the organization, and so on.

Zero-based budgets are also completed after major paradigm shifts. For example, suppose Medicare were to suddenly reimburse acute care hospital stays with a capitated reimbursement rate rather than a Diagnosis Related Group (DRG) rate. Reimbursement under Medicare under this new paradigm would be very different from the old paradigm, making this a good time for a healthcare organization to complete a zero-based budget. Completing a zero-based budget really forces organizations to justify every expense and reimbursement item.

Fixed Budgets

Organizations that are fiscally conservative generally adhere to a fixed budget. A fixed budget is prepared for the fiscal year, and this fixed budget never changes for that entire year. Variances of actual performance compared to the budget must be analyzed and justified. With a fixed budget, changes to performance management may occur, but changes to the budget will not.

UNDERSTANDING THE FISCAL YEAR

Generally, budgets are designed for a 1-year time period. This is known as the *fiscal year*. The fiscal year will vary from organization to organization. For example, in some states, the fiscal year begins on July 1 and ends on June 30. In other states, the fiscal year begins on January 1 and ends on December 31. Yet others have a fiscal year that begins on October 1 and ends on September 30.

The fiscal year for the Centers for Medicare & Medicaid Services (CMS), which is the administrative

continues >

office that administers the federal Medicare and Medicaid programs, is October 1 to September 30. This can create problems for some organizations. For example, if Medicare enacts a reduction in reimbursement on October 1, but a hospital's fiscal year ends on June 30 of the following year, this hospital may run into financial difficulty.

Flexible Budgets

A flexible budget is completed for a fiscal year, but is updated on a quarterly basis. For example, if patient volume has increased, staffing has most likely also increased; a flexible budget would be adjusted accordingly to account for this increased volume.

Historical Budgets

Most organizations complete annual historical budgets. A historical budget reviews prior years' data (the average daily census, hours per patient day, type of staffing, and so on). Based on the history of the organization, projections are made for the following fiscal year. The data in historical budgets can be used as baseline data.

Data from recent history is vital to the development of historical budgets. Usually, the first 8 months of operation are reviewed. A budget for the following year is then developed. Responsibility center managers review the proposed budgets and make recommendations and adjustments. Then, this budget is updated with information from months 9 and 10 of the current fiscal year.

RESPONSIBILITY CENTERS

A *responsibility center* is an organizational unit, area, or program. Some responsibility centers, such as pharmacies or laboratories, are revenue producing. These types of responsibility centers are often referred to as *revenue centers*. Other responsibility centers are nonrevenue producing, such as units that focus on environmental services or administration. These types of centers are often referred to as *cost centers*. A department might consist of one responsibility center or a combination of several responsibility centers. You'll learn more about responsibility centers in Chapter 5.

Operating Budgets Versus Capital Budgets

In addition to the types of budgets mentioned earlier in this chapter, there are two major categories of budgets for which nurse managers are held accountable:

> You should complete a zero-based budget as a check and balance on an organization's historical budget. This type of budget serves as a check and balance because it forces each expense item, as well as each revenue item, to be justified. Zero-based budgets do not rely on historical data.

- **Operating budget:** An *operating budget* is an overall plan for future operations, expressed in expense dollars and corresponding revenue dollars. An operating budget is a formal quantification of an organization's goals and objectives (a road map for achieving the organization's strategic mission, or the main reason the organization exists). The operating budget is one of management's most widely used tools. You'll learn more about operating budgets in Chapter 5.

PINPOINTING THE STRATEGIC MISSION

An organization's budget is intimately tied to the organization's strategic mission, and to the goals and objectives established by the organization to accomplish that mission. To create a budget, therefore, there must be a clear sense of the organization's strategic mission.

To pinpoint the organization's strategic mission, a clear understanding of the organization's goals and objectives is required. Accomplishing these goals and objectives will naturally lead to the fulfillment of the strategic mission. Of course, all this must be achieved in a cost-effective manner!

Organizations need to be transparent. Healthcare executives need to communicate the strategic vision and mission to all constituents within the organization.

- **Capital budget:** This budget is for major capital, or investment, expenditures (the purchase of new equipment, the construction of new facilities, and so on). You'll learn more about capital budgets in Chapter 6.

Summary

This chapter covered the following:

- Accrual basis of accounting
- Cash basis of accounting
- Assets, liability, and equity
- Responsibility center budgeting
- Zero-based budgets
- Flexible budgets
- Fixed budgets
- Historical budgets
- Operating budgets versus capital budgets
- Strategic vision and mission

4

Budget Development

Nurse managers set goals and design the budget (usually in collaboration with the finance department) for their own responsibility center, or nursing unit. After the budget has been developed and updated, it is submitted to administration and ultimately to the board of directors for approval. After the budget is approved and the fiscal year begins, the organization must deliver the planned services and programs.

> **NOTE**
>
> *The budgeting process is ongoing and dynamic. It should provide feedback; this is essential in managing the budget.*

The budget-development work flow involves the following steps:

1. Collecting relevant data

2. Planning services

3. Planning activities

4. Implementing the plan

5. Monitoring the budget

6. Taking corrective measures when necessary

NOTE

Spreadsheets, typically in Microsoft Excel, are used to calculate all budget components at the unit level.

Collecting Relevant Data

A critical task in creating a budget is collecting relevant data. The finance department ultimately collects the data, but this is done in collaboration with the nurse manager to create a functional budget. This includes the following information:

- **Services offered.** This data is collected by the nurse manager. That person knows best what services are currently offered and will be offered in the future. For example, a nurse manager may plan to increase bed capacity on an underutilized nursing unit as the census has increased the past year. The nurse manager knows that another surgeon is coming on staff who will bring increased volume to the facility, thus justifying the need for increasing the bed capacity.

- **Patient mix/case mix.** This pertains to the complexity of care. Generally, the more complex the case, the higher the reimbursement. Each hospital and nursing facility calculates an overall case-mix index. This is a number that is calculated by the finance department for the organization. The higher the number, the higher the reimbursement level.

- **Payer mix.** This number, also calculated by the finance department, reflects the patient demographics. For example, it might indicate that 50% of patients of a healthcare facility are below the age of 65 and have a managed care plan as their insurance plan. Generally, for such patients, length of stay is shorter, and reimbursement may be higher than for a Medicare patient. In contrast, this number might indicate that 70% of a facility's patients are over the age of 65 and that their primary insurance is Medicare. With Medicare, reimbursement is generally less than with commercial insurance companies, but length of stay is increased.

- **Acuity index.** The acuity index is a numeric calculation of the acuity of each patient on a given nursing unit. Once upon a time, there were level systems—for example, level 1 through 5, with 5 being the most complex case. The nurse manager or charge nurse on each shift would assign a numeric rank to each patient. A calculation was then done. The acuity index predicted the level of staffing required. Most of these systems were extremely inaccurate and almost always predicted a huge increase in staff that the organization could not afford. This was because the acuity index was always based on the subjectivity of the nurse completing the index. Today, computerized systems are used, which has significantly increased the accuracy of these systems.

In addition, the following data should be gathered:

- Hours provided per patient day

- Standards of care

- Plans for changes in services provided

- Plans for changes in resource utilization

All this information can be gleaned from the following data sources:

- **Historical information.** This data is composed of the prior years' history of operational performance found in budget reports. Information such as patient days, average length of stay, nursing hours per patient day, staff overtime, and so on are reviewed for prior years to make budget projections for the upcoming year.

> **NOTE**
>
> *Historical budgets can provide extremely useful information to plan the next year's budget. As a chief nursing officer (CNO), when I was planning the following year's budget, the finance department would always provide useful historical information. The facility that I worked for generally would provide information for the previous 4 to 5 years.*
>
> *Whenever data is provided, analysis of such data is critical. From reviewing the previous years' data, I could quickly identify patterns and trends. For example, were admissions increasing, decreasing, or remaining level? Was the patient's average length of stay increasing, decreasing, or remaining level? Once managed care kicked in it was very interesting to note how the length of stay of patients decreased. One of the data elements that I really homed in on was the nursing hours of care per patient day. From my experience speaking around the country, most facilities do make use of historical budgeting as a vital component of planning the next fiscal year's budget.*
>
> *Shorter time periods of history may be viewed when major paradigm shifts in healthcare reimbursement occur. For example, in my respective state, all insurance companies reimbursed acute inpatient hospital care under the DRG system as New Jersey was a waiver state secondary to being the first pilot state of the DRG system in the nation. Then in 1992, after a new governor was elected into office, he deregulated the healthcare insurance reimbursement industry in our state. Other than the federal system of reimbursement, that being Medicare, New Jersey became*

*like every other state. From 1992 on, all of the other
insurance companies negotiated rates with each hospital or
hospital system. 1992 was a pivotal year in our state as that
is considered the year that managed care was ushered into
our state. When those of us budgeting looked at historical
data, we could clearly see a difference in average length of
stay, admissions, and nursing hours per patient day after
1992. When we prepared a budget then for 1993 and 1994,
the information prior to 1992 was rather outdated as things
had changed. Other than Medicare, the state was under a
new reimbursement methodology, so it did not make sense
to track back that many years until the new system had
stabilized.*

- **Statistical reports/prior budget reports.** Statistical
  reports result from 1 year of operations in an
  organization. This year then becomes a prior year
  report and is part of the history of the organization.
  Most organizations do historical budgeting, so the
  finance department and the nurse manager refer to
  prior year reports when creating the budget for the
  next fiscal year.

- **Industry trends.** An example of an industry trend
  is a change in technology. For example, some
  orthopaedic total hip replacements now take an
  anterior approach, with the patient discharged the
  next day rather than enduring a 3-day hospital
  stay. This affects reimbursement. Another example
  is the use of percutaneous cardiac interventions
  rather than coronary bypass surgery in myocardial
  infarction patients. Other industry trends could relate
  to things happening in politics, such as decreasing
  reimbursement in the Medicare or Medicaid
  programs. Nurses need to be attuned to what the
  federal government does with federal insurance
  programs, as well as what their respective state
  government does with Medicaid, charity care, and
  other programs managed by the state.

- **Organizational goals and objectives.** Organizational goals and objectives are developed by the top administration. These are generally communicated to staff through their department directors and administrators. Nurse managers will formulate their own goals and objectives, which must be aligned with the overall organizational goals and objectives.

UNDERSTANDING THE CHART OF ACCOUNTS

During the budget-creation process, the financial department will establish what is known as a chart of accounts.

In accounting, the *chart of accounts* is a list of the names of income (revenue), expense (what the business spends), liability (what the business owes), and asset (what the business owns) accounts that a company uses in maintaining their books in a general ledger. The chart of accounts is set up by finance at the start of the business. Reference numbers are used to help classify the accounts by type. For example, in a hospital, each nursing unit will have a reference number. The chart organizes and tracks all of the business activities. Reports can then be easily generated in a logical sequence to track the financial history and progress of the business.

The chart of accounts does the following:

- It provides a format for the financial structure of the budget, so that all expenses and revenues can be tracked and recorded.

- It structures the recording and reporting of activities (revenue and expense).

- It organizes the information.

- It identifies the various areas of responsibility and the types of transactions that occur in each.

Here is how I view a chart of accounts, which sounds much more dramatic than what it really is. Think of a chart of accounts like your own household budget. My household budget is constructed with columns in a tabular format. In my household budget, I list all the revenue, that is, the income that I make from my primary job, practice as a nurse practitioner, consulting, etc. I then list all my expense items, for example, mortgage, car payment, electricity costs, gas costs, credit card bills, and other expense items. Each column has total amounts, for example, my total income from all that I do and my total expenses.

In a chart of accounts, the business's assets as well as liabilities are listed. I recently paid the mortgage off on the house so the house is now fully owned. I no longer need to list the mortgage amount as an expense. In my household budget I do not list my home as asset, even though it is. In comparison in a chart of accounts for a business, if the business fully owned the physical plant, the net worth of that plant would be listed as an asset. Liabilities are what the business owes, so they would also be listed in the chart of accounts.

Most nurse managers do not see nor prepare the chart of accounts. That is an accounting function of the finance department. However, it is important to know and realize that one does exist for a business.

Planning Services

Nursing is aware of what types of services will be rendered in the next fiscal year. Finance may be aware if it is a large project that the organization has been involved with, but many times finance is not aware of every type of service that will be rendered. For example, a nurse manager in an emergency department may be planning on opening a fast-track part of the emergency department to accommodate the minor emergencies more efficiently. This type of new service will require additional staffing. The budget will have to be formulated with this new service in mind. All associated costs, as well as projected volume and revenue, will need to be accounted for in the budget.

When you are planning a new service for the next fiscal budget, this needs to be communicated to the finance department. I always had an ongoing relationship with the finance department. It is crucial for nurse executives to embrace the concept of working well with the individuals in the organization who control the purse strings. I would meet biweekly with the budget manager. He would also meet with all of my managers on a biweekly basis. The purpose of these meetings was to review current finance reports, and these meetings also provided a communication forum for current and future activities and planning.

During budget preparation time, the budget manager from finance would also meet individually with my managers to plan the next fiscal year's budget. This also provided a mechanism for communicating any anticipated changes or additions in services.

Usually in a fiscal year there will be budget surprises. So how do these get communicated to finance? One example that happened to me was in the operating room. Laparoscopic surgical procedures were just beginning. Some of our medical staff had trained on this procedure and mid budget year they decided that they wanted to implement it. There were no huge costs associated with this; however, they were unplanned costs. New equipment needed to be purchased for the operating room. I then communicated this change with finance, the chief financial officer (CFO), and the chief executive officer (CEO). I explained that this would increase revenue in the long run and that we would lose market share if we did not implement this new procedure. We then as a united group sold this to the board of directors, who approved the purchase of the equipment for the implementation of this new procedure.

I think that what is important for mid budget year events is to really analyze what is requested. Some questions to consider are the following: Can it wait until the next fiscal year? Will market share be lost if we delay purchase or implementation? What are the overall costs? Do the costs outweigh the benefits? Will revenue increase?

Planning Activities

An activity may be a particular treatment that is new to the department. This will also have to be planned accordingly in the budget.

For example, when tissue plasminogen activator (TPA) was first available on the market to treat myocardial infarction patients in emergency departments, the cost of this medication was around $2,000 per treatment. The nurse manager would be aware of this new treatment, not the finance department. Let's say that this emergency department treats 2,000 myocardial infarction patients every year. Further, let's say that 75% of these patients *could* receive TPA.

The nurse manager needs to figure out how much cost this would be: (0.75 x 2,000 patients = 1,500 patients that could potentially receive TPA).

The costs would be: (1,500 patients x $2,000 per patient = $3,000,000.00 total costs).

If the nurse manager did not make finance aware of this new treatment and the associated costs, there would be a significant negative budget variance. Finance also would need to see if the insurances would reimburse this new treatment. You can see why the nurse manager is critical to planning activities for the budget.

DEFENDING YOUR PROPOSALS

Often, creating the budget involves defending what you have proposed. Nurse managers must be prepared to defend what they are proposing. It is a give-and-take process, based on the available resources of the organization.

Generally, the nursing department will estimate that more staffing and dollars will be needed to deliver care than what the finance group estimates. Given this, it's critical that nursing and finance come to agreement on the budget prior to presenting it to administration. Having these two departments in agreement becomes an item of defense if the CEO does not approve the budget as submitted.

The CEO will most likely question certain budgeted items. The item questioned most often is the care hours provided per patient day, because these hours convert to staffed hours. Usually, nursing attempts to increase the hours. Care hours provided should be in alignment with the complexity of the cases and the acuity system utilized (if any, because many healthcare facilities do not use acuity systems).

The best advice is to prepare for and anticipate questions. Back up information with data. Finance can help you in this preparation. For example, if you predict more care hours due to an increased census, demonstrate with data how the census has increased the past year. Demonstrate what percent occupancy your unit was at and for how long a time. Demonstrate how this trend will continue into the foreseeable future.

> **NOTE**
>
> *One of the challenging items to justify in a budget is a new nursing position, such as a new role. I really believe in the role of a clinical nurse specialist on a nursing unit. There is no doubt in my mind that a good clinical nurse specialist improves care and mentors and motivates nursing staff to excel. I was able to hire my first clinical specialist in maternal child health. This person was a dynamo who really improved care in this area. My vision was to have a clinical nurse specialist for every major service, for example, neuro, critical care, operating room, etc. Each year I would add a new clinical nurse specialist position to the budget. I had to justify this, but I utilized concrete outcome measurement from the clinical specialists in the role. This provided data that enabled me to get approval on these positions.*

Implementing the Plan

The budget plan is implemented by the nurse manager after approval by upper-level administration and ultimately the board of directors of the organization.

Implementing the plan means providing the services. For many nursing managers, this process will be no different from previous years. For some nurse managers, this might entail the implementation of new services or treatments. Implementation of the plan is really what occurs on a day-to-day basis with general operations of the organization (that is, the provision of care to patients). Budgeted expenses and revenue will be compared to actual expenses and revenue.

Monitoring the Budget

The budget must be monitored, with accurate financial reporting on a routine basis. It is the responsibility of the nurse manager and the finance department to monitor the budget. Using reports, you must compare actual revenue and expenses to the budgeted revenue and expenses. Variances must be identified. A variance analysis must be completed, where appropriate, to analyze cost, efficiency, and volume variances.

Variance analyses are completed whenever you have a deficit—that is, where actual expenses exceed budgeted expenses and where actual revenue is less than budgeted revenue. The variance analysis is completed so that the nurse manager knows exactly what is causing the problem. Armed with this knowledge, the nurse manager can take corrective action in the next budget cycle.

> **NOTE**
>
> *Variance analysis is discussed in more detail in Chapter 7.*

The finance department almost always completes these reports and sends them to the nurse manager for analysis and action. In some organizations the nurse manager may be completing a variance analysis and report. This will vary from organization to organization, but if it's the case for you, consult the finance department to learn the appropriate way to complete a variance report.

NOTE

To explore more about the various types of budget reports, see Chapter 8.

Taking Corrective Measures When Necessary

Based on performance, the initial goals may need to be modified. A change in the types and levels of services and the resources used may also be required.

As an example, let's return to the emergency department and review how the TPA administration to myocardial infarction patients is working out. Suppose that everything is going well and that the first quarter budget report is right on target with the budget, both from an expense side and a revenue side. In the second quarter, new evidence demonstrates that patients with an acute myocardial infarction ideally should be treated promptly in a cath lab so that percutaneous cardiac interventions can be performed (for example, an angioplasty with stent placement). During this second quarter, patients are now triaged right to the cardiac cath lab.

The budget projections are now not met with TPA secondary to this newer recommendation. The cath lab will need to change their budget for the next operating period as they are seeing a lot more cath patients. They will have to add staffing and more on-call shifts in their budget. The emergency department will need to downward adjust their projected cost and revenue for TPA as there are many fewer patients receiving TPA.

Management's Role in Budgeting

In terms of budgeting, management responsibilities are broken down as follows:

- **Department head.** Each department head or nurse manager is responsible for confirming the detailed operating expense budget for his or her department (cost center), consistent with organizational goals and objectives.

- **Director of budget.** The director of budget ensures that all budget forms are properly prepared and that data is accumulated within the specified timetable.

- **Vice presidents.** Vice presidents are responsible for the establishment of the basic annual budget formulation parameters. They assimilate departmental budgets into an organizational master budget consistent with organizational goals and objectives.

- **President/CEO.** The president or CEO has overall responsibility for the formulation and execution of the organization's budget. The president ensures consistency between the budget and divisional goals and objectives.

- **Finance committee and board of trustees.** These bodies are responsible for the review and approval of the completed operating budget.

In a healthcare setting, department heads and nurse managers are involved with some of the most critical functions in budgetary planning and the control process. They serve as the link between the plans of administration and the performance of the institution's workforce. If they fail to achieve the objectives and goals of the budget, the desired results will not be achieved.

SPOTTING A DYSFUNCTIONAL BUDGET

Budgets are viewed by managers as dysfunctional when they are considered to be any of the following:

- **Rigid.** Some fiscal departments are very conservative, and once the budget is created for the next year, it is more or less placed in stone. Variances are identified and explained, but the budget does not change for the entire year even though volume may have increased on a consistent basis.

- **Externally imposed.** A budget may be externally imposed by a higher administrative person (for example, a director of nursing). This person completes the budget with the finance budget manager and hands the budget down to nurse managers without their input. Another scenario could be that the nurse manager had input and recommended more staffing, but it is determined by higher administration that this staffing is not possible. Then the nurse manager must manage within the confines of the budget that was provided to him/her initially by the finance budget manager.

- **Interfering with interdepartmental/ intradepartmental cooperation and communication.** Departmental cooperation and communication can suffer when one department receives more in the budget compared to another department. For example, the nurse manager puts in a request in the capital budget for a new automatic blood pressure machine. This request is denied. The radiology department puts in a request for a new CT scanner, and this request

continues

is approved. The CT scanner is in the million-dollar range. The automatic blood pressure machine is in the thousand-dollar range. The nurse manager's working relationship with the radiology director suffers because of this.

- **Tools for which managers are held accountable but do not have the authority to control.** A nurse manager may be held accountable for the budget they do not have the authority to control. For example, in my very first management job I never saw the budget nor did I ever see budget reports. That was the job of the Director of Nursing. Two years into the job I got reprimanded for utilizing too much overtime. How could I know how much overtime I was using if I never saw a budget report? Thus, I was held accountable for the overtime, yet had no authority to really manage it and control it as I had no access to necessary reports.

Inventory Management

Inventory management refers to the overseeing and controlling of the ordering, storage, and use of supplies that a hospital or other healthcare organization will use in the provision of care. A hospital or healthcare organization's inventory is one of its major assets and represents an investment that is tied up until the item is used. It also costs money to store, track, and insure inventory. Inventories that are mismanaged can create significant financial problems for a healthcare entity, whether the mismanagement results in inventory excess or an inventory shortage.

Successful inventory management involves creating a purchasing plan that ensures that items are available when they are needed (but that neither too much nor too little is purchased) and keeping track of existing inventory and its use. Two common inventory-management strategies are as follows:

- **The just-in-time method.** Companies plan to receive items as they are needed rather than maintaining high inventory levels.

  An example of just-in-time inventory is ordering a very expensive surgical device that is rarely used and is ordered for a scheduled elective surgical procedure for a patient.

- **Materials requirement planning.** Companies schedule material deliveries based on projected forecasts.

The reality is that a lot of inventory in a hospital or other healthcare organization needs to be kept on hand for daily use. The amount kept available is based on prior experience and projected volumes for an upcoming fiscal cycle.

Inventory management also includes rotating stock, checking stock for outdated or near-outdated supplies, and making certain that supplies are on hand when needed.

Hospitals and healthcare organizations that fail to pay vendors for inventory can place the organization in jeopardy, as eventually the vendor will stop providing supplies to the hospital or healthcare organization.

One of the highest costs of inventory in a hospital is the operating room. In most operating rooms, surgeons have a procedure card for each type of surgical procedure that the respective surgeon performs. The procedure cards lists all the items or inventory required for the procedure.

Hospitals often design their informatics system so that when the nurse pulls the inventory for the procedure, the system automatically bills the patient's account and orders replacement inventory. This system definitely ensures that the correct amount of inventory is on hand and that the correct party is billed for the used inventory. This system also controls costs because items are replaced when used and excessive inventory is not maintained.

DEALING WITH INVENTORY ISSUES

An emergency department nurse manager who managed a busy inner-city emergency department was checking the supply room for Lactated Ringer's on a Friday afternoon, because this emergency department usually experienced a large number of trauma patients on a Friday evening. The nurse manager noticed that there were no bags of Lactated Ringer's on the shelf. The nurse manager called the central processing department that stocked the supplies, questioning why there were no Lactated Ringer's on the shelf. The response was that they had run out of Lactated Ringer's. On further exploration, the nurse manager learned that the hospital was experiencing financial difficulty and had not been paying their vendors. The vendor that supplied the Lactated Ringer's would not send more bags of Lactated Ringer's until they received a payment.

Vendor disputes need to be addressed prior to a problem developing, such as the emergency department not having Lactated Ringer's solution on hand. A well-functioning purchasing department would not have allowed such an event to occur. Certain vendors must be paid in a timely manner for critical supplies to be available. Can you imagine what would happen if the company that supplied the hospital's oxygen was not paid and no oxygen was delivered?

The key is to negotiate reasonable charges. This can be done in several ways. One way certainly is to explore how many companies make a particular item and then get price quotes. Hospitals working together in a network can have a huge impact on lowering costs. For example, if 10 hospitals network with each other for group purchasing, and a company refuses to lower costs, most likely another company would be more than happy to do so as they would gain 10 hospitals' business.

In the case example of the emergency department, this was a two hospital system and the other hospital had extra Ringer's Lactate solution on hand so they sent some over to the hospital without the Ringer's Lactate solution. Other crystalloid solutions could also be utilized on an emergency basis, such as normal saline solution.

Summary

This chapter discussed the following steps of the budget-development work flow:

- Collecting data
- Planning services
- Planning activities
- Implementing the plan
- Monitoring the budget
- Taking corrective measures when necessary
- Management's role in budgeting
- Inventory management

5

Building Operating Budgets

As mentioned earlier in this book, the operating budget is the overall plan for future operations, expressed in expense dollars and corresponding revenue dollars. The operating budget attempts to consider all the revenues and expenses of the organization. Of course, the goal is to have revenues exceed expenses. Management action is critical to managing the budget. The creation of the operating budget should be a joint effort by the administration and management teams.

Budgeting is a process for converting an operating plan into financial terms by outlining resources to achieve the goals and objectives of the organization. It is a managerial tool that is driven by strategy, goals and objectives, and trends in the industry. The budget provides the organization with a financial road map.

The rationale for budgeting is to prep an organization for the future, to communicate expectations regarding the operating functions of the organization, and to allocate resources among the competing demands that occur within the organization.

Performance management is a critical component of the budget process. Performance management consists of a defined process that evaluates actual expenses from operations and compares that to budgeted expenses for the same time period, which can be biweekly, monthly, quarterly, and annually. Should a difference or variance be demonstrated, appropriate strategies can be taken by the organization in a timely manner to rectify the variance. Difficult parameters to assess can be volume (too high or too low), market conditions, and seasonality; for instance, snow can cause accidents, which then increases the volume.

There are three major types of budgets:

- As previously stated, the operating budget consists of all revenue and expenses for the day-to-day operations of the organization.

- The capital budget consists of fixed assets and major movable equipment with useful life generally that will last longer than a 2-year time period. The amount budgeted for major movable equipment will vary from organization to organization.

- The cash budget estimates future cash receipts and payments that are tabulated to demonstrate the forecasted cash balance.

ANALYZING BUDGET DIFFERENCES

A new vaccine to prevent Ebola is being implemented. Anyone over the age of 2 can receive the vaccine.

The vaccine costs $100 per person to administer. The cost of the vaccine to the healthcare organization is $75 per dose. The net revenue per vaccine administration should be $25 per injection.

Expenses were up for the first time period that the vaccine was administered. How could you analyze the root cause of the budget difference? Questions to consider might include the following:

- Did volume increase: Did more individuals access the vaccination?

- Was a more expensive vaccine utilized than initially planned?

- Was more revenue received to offset the expenses incurred?

It is important for nurse managers to analyze when expenses increase. At times this increase can be good. Certainly, when more individuals access vaccines than anticipated, that is a good thing as in the long run fewer individuals should become ill, thus contributing to a cost savings as well as better health outcomes for patients.

The operating budget projects anticipated activities and the resources required to support the planned activity. It is a projection of revenues and expenses for a given time period (usually 1 year). It has a framework within the financial structure and reporting mechanisms of the organization.

Specifically, the operating budget is based on the following:

- Anticipated levels of output, in terms of the following:

  - The number of admissions

  - The number of patient days

  - Departmental activity

  - New services/programs

- Predetermined hospital goals and objectives

- Agreement with the strategic/long-range plan

NOTE

All nurse managers must consider their unit a mini business center, each with its own characteristics and needs.

Key Metrics in the Operating Budget

A key metric for managers when creating the operating budget is the workload for the next year. *Workload* is the amount of work performed by a unit, and is often measured in units of service. *Units of service* are used to determine revenues and resource requirements.

To calculate this, one must gather key statistics concerning current activity. These include the following:

- **Census:** This refers to the number of beds occupied every day, usually at midnight.

- **Occupancy rate:** This is the percentage of the total number of beds filled.

- **Average daily census (ADC):** This is the number of patients cared for each day on average, over a specific period of time. To obtain this statistic, simply divide the number of patients seen by the number of days in the specific time period.

- **Average length of stay (ALOS):** This is the average number of days that one is an inpatient. To obtain this statistic, divide the number of inpatient days by the total number of patients.

Of course, another critical metric is revenue. Once upon a time, nurse managers were not privy to the revenue side of the equation. The thinking in the finance department was that if nurse managers were not made aware of the revenue, they would not know whether the organization was making money or losing money. As a result, the finance department could always push nurse managers to control or cut expenses.

Today, the opposite is true. Now, most nursing managers in the vast majority of organizations *do* see the revenue side of the equation. Nurse managers are urged to think of their responsibility center or unit as their own business, with the goal of maximizing profits.

> **NOTE**
>
> *For individual responsibility centers, the revenue listed on the financial report generally reflects only the gross charges for services provided by that area.*

Sources of revenue include the following:

- Patient service revenue
  - Gross patient service revenue (GPSR): Revenue received from the provision of health services to patients, inclusive of both inpatient and outpatient revenue.

- Net patient service revenue (NPSR): The estimated net revenue that the organization actually sees. For example, an insurance company may deny some procedures or services. Net revenue also results from contracted allowances, which are discounts that the organization has agreed to with the insurance company and other third-party payers through negotiated contracts or agreements. Patients cannot be billed the difference for such circumstances.

- Payment for inpatient treatment and care

- Payment for outpatient treatment and care

Other revenue to consider includes dollars earned from the cafeteria, gift shop, parking fees, and investment income.

Bad debt consists of expected revenue for services rendered but that the organization did not receive. This results from insurance companies and other third-party payers not approving payment for services and from patients failing to make their copayments or pay for services not covered by the insurance company or the third-party payer.

Charity care is a program that some states implement. It may or may not cover all or part of services based on criteria (for example, financial need, geographic region, and other indicators). Generally, charity care is recorded as a reduction in revenue, and bad debt is recorded as an expense.

Revenue is based on the prices, or charges, set for specific services. The sum of all charges is the gross patient revenue. As mentioned previously, almost no one pays full charges:

- Medicare pays a fixed amount per inpatient, based on the discharge diagnosis.

- Medicaid generally pays less than the stated charges, with the amount varying from state to state.

- Third-party payers, or insurance companies, pay a negotiated discounted rate, called the *contractual allowance*.

- Charity care is provided by most institutions to some degree.

It follows, then, that net revenue is the key metric here. To obtain the net revenue, use the following simple formula.

$$Gross\ Revenue$$
$$-\ Deductions\ from\ Revenue$$
$$=\ Net\ Revenue$$

Calculating the net revenue.

THE RED AND THE BLACK

The difference between the amount collected from payers, patients, and other sources, and the amount hospitals spend to provide care, is called the *operating margin*. When revenue exceeds expenses (the goal), an organization is said to have a black bottom line. A red bottom line is when expenses exceed revenue, and the organization has lost money.

Understanding Expenses

For individual responsibility centers, expenses listed on financial reports are generally direct expenses (that is, expenses tied to the activity in that responsibility center).

The two main types of direct expenses are as follows:

- **Direct patient care costs:** Examples of direct patient care costs include staff nurse salaries, dressing supplies, IV fluids, and so on.

- **Indirect patient care costs:** These are specific to supporting the overall operation of the area. Examples of indirect patient care costs include seminars, conferences or continuing education hours, office supplies, and so on. Indirect patient care costs also include costs shared by all departments, such as lighting, heating, administrative, and other personnel costs.

Expenses are also sorted into employment costs (also called salary-related expenses) and nonsalary expenses. Employment costs are categorized as follows:

- **Type of employee:** Types might include doctor, RN, patient care tech, pharmacist, pharmacy tech, and so on.

- **Type of hours paid:** Examples include regular time, overtime, vacation hours, holiday hours, sick hours, and so on.

- **Types of differential paid:** Examples include shift differential, on-call pay, and so on.

- **Benefits paid:** Examples include health insurance, FICA, matching 401(k) (rare today), and so on.

Examples of nonsalary expenses include the following:

- Office supplies

- Major movable equipment

- Professional journal subscriptions

- Instruments

- General patient care supplies

In addition to these are expenses incurred by a department and charged to the patient. These include the following:

- Telephone calls

- Internet connection

- Stock medications
- Central supplies
- Linen supplies

NOTE

The percentage difference between expenses and revenue is called the profit margin. In today's economic climate, it is becoming more difficult for healthcare organizations to have a positive profit margin.

IDENTIFYING THE BREAK-EVEN POINT

The point at which revenue covers cost is called the *break-even point*. The break-even point is usually represented on a graph with two diagonal lines. In this graph, one line represents revenue and the other line represents expense; the break-even point is where both lines intersect (see Figure 5.1).

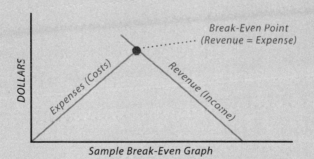

Sample Break-Even Graph

FIGURE 5.1
The break-even point.

Projecting Expenses

To project nonsalary expenses, an organization usually reviews 8 months of actual performance in a given year, and then updates the budget to the last 2 months of the year. After actual expenses are analyzed, any expense not considered appropriate is not included in the projection base. Such expenses include the following:

- Expenses in excess of the budget not considered to be reasonable

- One-time expenses not expected to occur in the following budget year

- Prior-year expenses unrelated to current operating expenses

Economic factors must also be considered. For example, projecting Diagnosis Related Group (DRG) reimbursement rates for the following budget year may still be based on established DRG rates from 3 or more years past. Often, costs are adjusted only for inflationary factors rather than for increased rates themselves.

Estimated inflation factors, or economic factors, are usually developed by each respective state (for example, the state department of health) for all major expense categories. These expense categories include the following:

- Salaries

- Benefits

- Supplies

- Pharmaceuticals

- Food

Requests for additional budgeted dollars can be met with other departmental savings. Nurse managers must consider various methods to increase productivity and work efficiency in the face of current economic trends and cost containment.

NOTE

The biggest impact on the budget is nurse staffing. Nurse managers must increase productivity by staffing to the planned hours of nursing care and by not exceeding those hours of care. This implies that nurse managers must flex staffing with both the patient census and the acuity of the patients.

Productive Versus Nonproductive Nursing Hours

Productive hours are actual direct hours work. The hours are hours that the nurse is performing nursing activities in the presence of a patient on a nursing unit.

Example of productive hours include the following:

- Medication administration
- Nursing treatments
- Admitting a patient
- Transferring a patient
- Discharging a patient
- Patient education
- Communication with the patient
- Coordinating patient care
- Documentation of patient care either handwritten or electronically
- Treatment planning time

Exclusions include the following:

- Holiday time
- Vacation time
- Sick time
- Bereavement time
- Orientation time
- Committee time

EXAMPLE OF PRODUCTIVE WORK HOURS

Hospital XYZ implemented Jean Watson's theory of caring and relationship-based care. One of the nursing units implemented the "caring moment." The "caring moment" involved the nurse proactively spending 10 to 15 minutes each day explaining to the patient what would be occurring that day (for example, what tests the patient would have). The nurse also took this time to ask patients if they had any questions or concerns and whether the patients needed her to address anything.

The time that nurse spent communicating with the patient would be consider productive hours worked.

Calculating Employee-Related Costs

The nursing department is usually the largest cost center in any hospital. Given that, and the fact that the provision of healthcare is a service industry, it should come as no surprise that employees account for the greatest expense in a healthcare organization. For this reason, budget preparation in a healthcare setting usually begins with the employees.

The first task is to determine how many employees are needed in a given responsibility center. To calculate required employees, you must obtain the following information:

- **The average daily census (ADC) for the responsibility center:** As mentioned, the ADC is the number of patients cared for each day on average, over a specific period of time. To obtain this statistic, first add together census figures for each day in the given period. Then divide that total by the number of days.

Total Census Figures
÷ Total Number of Days
= ADC

Calculating the ADC.

- **The average monthly patient days:** To obtain this statistic, multiply the average daily census by the number of days in the calendar year (365). Then divide the product of that calculation by the number of months in the year (12).

(ADC x 365) ÷ 12
= Average Monthly Patient Days

Calculating the average monthly patient days.

- **The number of hours of nursing care to be provided:** To calculate this, multiply the total patient days per year by the hours of care per patient per day to be budgeted.

Total Patient Days per Year
x Hours of Care per Patient per Day
= Hours of Nursing Care to be Provided

Calculating the number of hours of nursing care to be provided.

- **The hours of care per patient day to be budgeted:** The hours of care per patient per day to be budgeted is determined by the nurse manager, based on the standards of care that he or she wants to provide.

- **Hours per patient day:** The hours of nursing care provided per patient per day (over 24 hours) by various levels of nursing personnel (e.g., RN, LPN, nursing care tech).

Hours of Nursing Care Provided per Patient per Day
x Various Levels of Nursing Personnel
= Hours of Care per Day to be Budgeted

Calculating the number of hours of care
per patient to be budgeted.

- **The total hours of care delivered:** This is the total actual patient days for a year multiplied by the hours of care per patient day.

Total Patient Days for a Year
x Hours of Care per Patient Day
= Total Hours of Care Delivered

Calculating the total hours of care delivered.

This information will dictate the number of full-time employees (FTEs) required to do the job.

Calculating the Number of FTEs Needed

By definition, an FTE works 2,080 hours per year (generally, 8 hours per day, 5 days per week). To calculate the total FTE requirements, then, you divide the total hours of care to be delivered per year by the hours worked by one FTE per year (2,080). So, for example, if the total hours of care to be delivered were 146,000, you would divide that number by 2,080, for a result of 70.192. In other words, 70.192 FTEs would be needed to provide 146,000 hours of care.

Total Hours of Care to be Delivered per Year
÷ Hours Worked by One FTE per Year (2,080)
= Number of FTEs Needed

Calculating the number of FTEs needed.

> **NOTE**
>
> *More than one employee can compose one FTE. For example, two part-time employees, each working 20 hours, would compose one FTE.*

Accounting for Benefit Time

There is a problem with this calculation: It did not account for employee benefit, or nonproductive, time. Every organization administers benefit time differently. Examples of benefit time include the following:

- Vacation time
- Holiday time
- Sick time

- Bereavement time
- Education/conference hours
- Family medical leave

For example, suppose a healthcare organization offers full-time employees the following benefit time:

- 10 vacation days
- 10 holidays
- 10 sick days
- 3 bereavement days

That adds up to 33 days off per year. When developing a budget, you should assume that every employee will take all their benefit time in that fiscal year (even though a lot of employees do not).

When accounting for benefit time, you must convert the benefit days to hours. Regardless of what shift an employee works, benefit time is always calculated as an 8-hour day. To convert the benefit days to hours, you multiply the number of benefit days by 8. So, in this example, 33 benefit days equals 264 total benefit hours.

Total Number of Benefit Days
x 8
= Total Benefit Hours

Converting benefit days to benefit hours.

After you convert the benefit days to hours, you must subtract those benefit hours from the 2,080 hours generally worked by an FTE. This yields each FTE's productive hours worked. In this example, employees' productive hours worked equals 264 subtracted from 2,080, or 1,816).

2,080
– Total Benefit Hours
= Productive Hours Worked

Calculating productive hours worked.

Finally, you must divide the total staffed hours (in this example, 146,000) by the productive time (here 1,816 hours). The result: 80.39 (a much higher number than the 70.192 noted in the preceding section). In other words, an additional 10 FTEs are required to cover for employees when they take their benefit time. If a nursing manager did not go this extra step, that nursing unit would always be short-staffed or would have to be covered by overtime staff or agency staff, which might not be in budget.

Other Key Calculations

As you develop your budget, you'll need to keep a few other formulas in mind:

- **Annual nursing hours:** You calculate this by multiplying the projected patient days in a year by the hours of nursing care per patient per day. The annual nursing hours translate to dollars when the average hourly salary rate is factored in.

Projected Patient Days per Year
x Hours of Nursing Care per Patient per Day
= Annual Nursing Hours

Calculating annual nursing hours.

- **Annual payroll costs:** To calculate this, multiply the average hourly rate by the annual staffed hours. (Hourly rates are set by the human resources department and the average per unit is calculated by finance.) Annual payroll costs are generally at least 70% of the total budget for nursing. Nursing is a service department, and therefore, payroll costs are the most significant dollars expended.

Average Hourly Rate
x Annual Staffed Hours
= Annual Payroll Costs

Calculating annual payroll costs.

- **Annual benefit costs:** To calculate this, multiply annual payroll costs by the benefit percentage. Every organization provides benefits, and these benefits have a cost. In most healthcare organizations, the benefit package is somewhere between 25% and 30%, or more. (The actual number depends on the organization, and is furnished by the human resources department.) When doing a budget, the cost of employee benefits must be factored in because it is a significant dollar amount.

Annual Payroll Costs
x Benefit Percentage
= Annual Benefit Costs

Calculating annual benefit costs.

- **Total annual payroll costs:** You calculate this by adding the annual payroll costs with the annual benefit costs. Payroll costs are the largest piece of the nursing operating budget.

$$Annual\ Payroll\ Costs\ +\ Annual\ Benefit\ Costs$$
$$=\ Total\ Annual\ Payroll\ Costs$$

Calculating total annual payroll costs.

Putting It All Together

Table 5.1 shows a sample personnel budget for a nursing unit. Take note of the formulas next to each item in the table.

TABLE 5.1

FIXED PERSONNEL BUDGET FOR NURSING UNIT

Total bed capacity	50
Projected occupancy	80%
Projected average daily census	40
Projected annual patient days	14,600 (40 x 365 days/year)
Average nursing hours per patient day	10 hours per patient day per 24-hour period
Annual nursing hours (staffed hours)	146,000 (14,600 x 10)
Average hourly wage	$30
Annual salary costs minus benefits	$4,380,000 (146,000 x 30)
Benefits at 30% salary costs	$1,314,000 (0.30 x 4,380,000)
Total annual personnel (payroll) costs	$5,694,000 (4,380,000 + 1,314,000)
Average monthly patient days	1,216.7 (14,600 ÷ 12)
Average monthly nursing hours	12,166.7 (146,000 ÷ 12)
Average monthly personnel costs	$474,500.00 (5,694,000 ÷ 12)

Table 5.2 shows a flexible budget. In this example, a manager prepared three budgets based on variable census levels. Take note of the bold items, which do not change regardless of the census.

TABLE 5.2
FLEXIBLE PERSONNEL BUDGET FOR NURSING UNIT

	Census X	Census Y	Census Z
Total bed capacity	**50**	**50**	**50**
Projected occupancy	70%	80%	90%
Projected average daily census	35	40	45
Projected annual patient days	12,775	14,600	16,425
Average nursing hours per patient day (PPD)	10 hours PPD	10 hours PPD	10 hours PPD
Annual nursing hours (staffed hours)	127,750	146,000	164,250
Average hourly wage	**$30.00**	**$30.00**	**$30.00**
Annual salary costs minus benefits	$3,832,500	$4,380,000	$4,927,500
Benefits at 30% of salary costs	$1,149,750	$1,314,000	$1,478,250
Total annual personnel (payroll) costs	$4,982,250	$5,694,000	$6,405,750

Bold items do not change regardless of census data.

Outpatient Reimbursement

Outpatient activity represents a growing percentage of total patient revenue in most hospitals. This is especially true since the Patient Protection and Affordable Care Act (ACA) was passed in 2010, which represents a shift in focus from acute care and interventional services to that of health promotion and primary care.

Technology also plays a factor in how care is delivered as there are many more noninvasive or less invasive procedures being done in outpatient settings. Managed care also has fostered growth in the outpatient arena. Outpatient revenue is received from radiology, laboratory, infusion, other services, and some outpatient ancillaries related to hospital-based visits.

Outpatient care is generally characterized by high volume with lower revenue. Outpatient revenue can also be more difficult to estimate and analyze.

The Outpatient Prospective Payment System (OPPS) is similar in nature to the Diagnosis Related Group (DRG) system utilized by Medicare for inpatient hospital care. OPPS is classified into groups termed Ambulatory Payment Classifications (APCs). Depending on the services rendered, a hospital may be paid for more than one APC encounter. Established fee schedules are payer specific. Payment is made for services such as the following:

- Laboratory
- Radiology
- Emergency department
- Clinic visits
- Ambulatory categories

The fee schedule also includes both a technical and a professional component. The technical fee schedule is for hospital services. The professional fee schedule is for physicians and other health providers providing services in an office-based setting or for hospital staff physicians and healthcare providers providing such a service in a hospital outpatient setting. Items that are not listed or categorized in the established fee schedule will typically default to a percent of charges as a payment methodology.

Busting Budget Myths

When it comes to budgeting, myths abound. Here are some common budget myths:

- **The more money you spend this year, the more money will be allocated in your budget next year.** Based on current reimbursement trends, the opposite is true. That is, the more money a nurse manager spends this year, the *less* money will be allocated in next year's budget. Worse, by spending too much money, the nurse manager may actually be hastening the organization's demise.

- **Every vacant FTE position must be filled ASAP.** Once upon a time, filling every vacated FTE immediately was important. If the nurse manager failed to do this, the finance department would most likely eliminate that FTE in the next year's budget, assuming the position was unnecessary because it had not been filled. Today, a nurse manager views a vacated FTE as an opportunity to reduce expenses and keep the organization whole (financially speaking), without having to resort to layoffs.

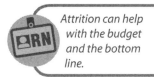
Attrition can help with the budget and the bottom line.

- **Do not be under budget; otherwise, your budget for the next year will be decreased.** Again, once upon a time, this myth was reality. A nursing manager who managed his or her unit prudently usually got penalized in the end. The finance department would view such a manager as efficient. That is, if the unit ran with less this year, it was assumed that it could do so next year. Today, a good, prudent nurse manager does try to run his or her unit under budget. Nurse managers have become much more effective at variance analysis and productivity, optimizing revenue over expenses.

- **The state will always bail you out.** I had this feeling as a new nurse manager. Heck, I even had it as a nurse executive! I thought the government would never let a hospital close. Guess what? Local, state, and national governments *do* let hospitals close. Perhaps the best example is Saint Vincent Hospital in downtown Manhattan. Whoever could have dreamed that hospital would close? But it did. In my state, we have experienced 27 hospital closures to date, and many others are in jeopardy, losing money, or have declared bankruptcy.

Summary

This chapter discussed the following:

- Development of the operating budget
- Key formulas that are necessary to construct and understand the operating budget
- Metrics utilized in development of the operating budget
- Sample operating budgets
- Common budget myths
- Performance management
- Gross and net patient service revenue
- Productive and nonproductive nursing hours
- Outpatient reimbursement

6

Capital Budgets

The small hospital where I worked when I graduated from nursing school was a community facility. Although the hospital staff offered excellent care, I couldn't help but notice the hospital's outdated equipment and leaky roof.

After several years of financial troubles, the hospital closed. I quickly realized that the facility's closure was directly related to its physical condition. Clearly, those in charge of the hospital had failed to budget for the state-of-the-art equipment and facilities that patients in the United States customarily expect.

The budgets for these types of items are called *capital budgets*. Capital budgets, which are an important part of long-range and strategic planning, are used to budget for major movable equipment and fixed assets. Items in a capital budget typically have a lifetime exceeding the year of purchase. They are generally major investments; it takes a long time to recover their costs.

Why is a separate budget required for capital purchases? Because items in capital budgets are expensive.

Also, they last a long time. Perhaps most important, the return on the investment in capital items will be seen over several years, not just the year of purchase.

Budgeting for Major Movable Equipment

The capital budget for major movable equipment includes items that are expected to last for longer than 1 year, but that will not be a permanent fixture in the organization. For example, computers, which generally last 3 years on average, are considered major movable equipment. Other examples include the following:

- Automatic blood pressure machines

- CT scanners and MRI machines

- Portable cardiac transport monitors

- Automatic external defibrillators (AEDs)

- Stretcher beds

Capital items placed in the budget will vary based on the minimum dollar amount of items that must be included in the budget. This minimum amount will vary from organization to organization.

> **NOTE**
>
> *Information technology–related purchases are excellent examples of capital budget items. Most healthcare organizations are spending significant amounts of money on IT. The trend toward electronic health records is driving the need for such items to be placed in the capital budget.*

Budgeting for Fixed Assets

In addition to budgeting for major movable items in the capital budget, you must consider fixed assets. Fixed assets are stationary. They do not move. A renovation of a conference center might appear in the capital budget as a fixed asset, as might a new building. Organizations can also purchase real estate for current or future growth and development. Such purchases are also considered fixed assets.

NOTE

Nurse managers would be involved with such budgeting if, for example, their nursing unit were going to be renovated.

Examples of Capital Expenditures

Capital expenditures include the following:

- **Capital investments.** This is money that is invested in the business with the end result of producing income through earnings that are generated by the business over a several-year time period. This money is expected to be utilized for capital expenditures rather than day-to-day operational expenses.

- **Long-term investments.** Long-term investments are items that a company intends to hold onto for more than a 1-year time period. Examples include stocks, bonds, real estate, and cash.

- **Capital assets.** These include land and buildings.

- **Capital acquisitions.** An acquisition is any good or service purchased for the business. Examples include stock for resale, items required to produce a product or supply a service, advice, or costs associated with the lease or hire of premises or business-related equipment.

- **Capital items.** As mentioned, examples of capital items include automatic blood pressure machines, CT scanners and MRI machines, portable cardiac transport monitors, AEDs, and stretcher beds.

In some organizations, any items over $1,000 should appear in the capital budget. In others, that dollar amount may differ, ranging from $350 to $5,000. (Note that this dollar amount tends to rise with inflation.)

> **NOTE**
>
> *Organizations that place items costing less than $1,000 on the capital budget tend to be very fiscally conservative—not necessarily a bad thing in today's economy!*

Why Develop a Capital Budget?

Why develop a capital budget? Lots of reasons. Here are a few:

- **To improve quality for patients/staff.** When equipment and technology are not replaced or updated, patients and staff can be negatively impacted. Think about it: Would you want to have a testing procedure done where the latest technology was not available and not utilized?

- **To improve safety for patients/staff.** Generally, more state-of-the-art technology provides improved safety for patients and staff.

- **To add new or update current technology.** For example, you might purchase an item to bring the institution to the level of a state-of-the-art facility.

- **To improve productivity.** In addition to helping staff work more efficiently, some equipment may allow for the replacement of high-priced human labor.

- **To replace an older item with a similar updated item.** As stated, when equipment and technology are not replaced or updated, patients and staff can feel negative impacts. For example, with older defibrillators, whenever someone used a synchronized cardioversion, there was quite a delay in the machine sensing the R wave on the ECG cycle, and hence, a delay in the delivery of the shock. In contrast, with today's defibrillators, when someone employs synchronized cardioversion, the sensing of the R wave on the ECG cycle (and therefore the release of the shock) is almost instantaneous, due to advanced micro computer chips.

Developing the Capital Budget

Developing a capital budget is a matter of determining what capital purchases should be made. These purchases could be direct or indirect:

- **Direct purchases.** Direct purchases have a clear impact on the care provided or the workload involved. An example of a direct purchase is when an organization purchases a piece of equipment. When the equipment arrives, the care provided is directly impacted.

- **Indirect purchases.** Indirect purchases have an indirect impact on the care provided or the workload involved. Examples of indirect purchases include spare parts, maintenance materials, such as lubricants for machinery, and operating supplies.

NOTE

With capital expenditures, organizations commit to a multiyear relationship. The longer the acquisition will be around, the more scrutiny will be applied to its purchase.

To determine what items to include in a capital budget, start by maintaining inventories of major movable equipment. Then, for each piece of equipment, ask the following questions:

- What is the expected useful life of this piece of equipment?

- What is its anticipated depreciation value (see the following sidebar)?

- How often is this piece of equipment utilized?

- Is this piece of equipment outdated?

- When was this equipment last replaced?

- When should it be replaced again?

Answering these questions will help you determine when various pieces of equipment should be budgeted for in the capital budget.

A WORD ON DEPRECIATION

Capital items depreciate over time. When budgeting capital items, you must consider the depreciation value. Depreciation spreads the cost of an item out over each useful year of an item's life. Although the capital acquisition itself will appear in the capital budget only in the year it is purchased, the depreciation costs will be identified in each year's operating budget for the life of the item.

Information about depreciation can be obtained by the nurse manager in a couple ways:

- The manufacturer of the piece of equipment may indicate that item's expected life. For example, it is generally accepted that computer technology must be replaced every 3 years or so due to changes in technology and the expected shelf life of most computers.

- The organization may define depreciation time in capital items where the depreciation time is not established or is unclear. This time frame can also be based on the reality of what the organization can afford over time.

It is always best for a nurse manager to first check with the manufacturer to see what the expected life of the piece of equipment is. The nurse manager should also check with the finance budget manager.

Also, remember that although equipment may last a long time, practice guidelines may change, thus necessitating a change in the depreciation time and value. For example, where I practice, the organization purchased an AED. The AED was programmed to the 2000 advanced cardiac life support (ACLS) guidelines, where three consecutive stacked shocks were recommended for a patient in ventricular fibrillation. This AED still works, but in 2005, the ACLS guidelines changed to one shock at maximum setting every 2 minutes, not the three consecutive shocks previously recommended. In that case, if the manufacturer of the AED did not have an updated computer module to change the settings of the AED, a new AED would need to be purchased, even though the old AED works perfectly fine.

CAPITAL BUDGET MAJOR MOVABLE EQUIPMENT: NONINVASIVE BLOOD PRESSURE MONITORING DEVICE

Healthcare organizations generally base their equipment decisions on a few factors. One is depreciation value. The other major factor is useful life of the item. Over time most items depreciate in monetary value as well as useful life. To make a comparison consider a refrigerator that you may purchase today. If the refrigerator costs $2,000.00 and is expected to last around 10 years, then this item depreciates $200.00 each year. Ideally you should plan to save $200.00 a year for 10 years so that if the refrigerator no longer functions after 10 years, you would then have the money saved to purchase a new refrigerator. When planning a capital budget for major movable equipment, you should plan to replace an item (even if it is still working) when the useful lifetime has been met. This assures that an organization will always have state-of-the-art equipment.

The following table provides an example of a major movable equipment item (in this case a noninvasive blood pressure monitoring device) in a capital budget. The item described has an expected useful life of 5 years, so ideally in year 5 a new item should be placed in the capital budget.

Year of Purchase	Cost	$1,000
Year 1	Depreciation	$200
Year 2	Depreciation	$200
Year 3	Depreciation	$200
Year 4	Depreciation	$200
Year 5	Depreciation	$200
Total	Total Depreciation Value in Year 5	$1,000

In this scenario, the plan would be to purchase a new noninvasive blood pressure monitor in year 5.

PLANNING AHEAD FOR THE FOLLOWING YEAR

If you're responsible for developing a capital budget, you want to get into the habit of thinking ahead. In addition to building your budget for this year, start a list for the following year, too. For example, if you've proposed an item for this year's capital budget, but that item has been deemed nonessential in the short term, you might add that item to your capital budget for the following year, at which point its purchase will become more critical.

In addition, you should survey your staff. Ask them what equipment they believe is necessary to do their job, improve care given to patients, and ensure their own safety. Because nurse managers must work to retain staff, those capital items that help nurses do their job better or otherwise benefit them are often worth pursuing.

When considering an item for the capital budget, managers must examine the alternatives. That is, could a similar item be purchased for less money? Might there be other, less expensive ways to achieve the same results? Successful capital budgets evaluate alternative plans and purchases. The capital budget should not be just a wish list of items.

NOTE

It is not unusual for a capital purchase to result in a couple years of negative cash flow.

Perhaps most important, the purchase should yield a tangible economic return. When evaluating an item, ask the following questions:

- Will the capital purchase price be offset by the anticipated revenue from the purchase?

- What will be the clinical impact of the capital acquisition?

- Is there a quality issue here? That is, does the purchase price exceed the proposed revenue, but improve the overall quality of care?

- What will be the impact of the purchase on the staff?

- Will the staff's work life improve as a result of the purchase?

- Will labor hours be saved a result of the purchase?

- Will the purchase help make money for the organization?

APPRECIATING ITEMS

Fixed assets, which are another part of a capital budget, are a good example of appreciation value. Fixed assets are stationary items, for example, renovating an educational classroom. Costs will be initially high. This asset is fixed, that is, a room is not movable. This asset will also not be replaced for the foreseeable future. An excellent example of a fixed asset that appreciates is a real estate purchase. Many hospitals purchase properties around the hospital campus, oftentimes for future expansion. Generally real estate purchases increase or appreciate in value over time.

Inevitably, you'll have to justify items in your capital budget to personnel in your facility's finance department and/or to a capital review committee. When the time comes, you want the following information on hand:

- A description of the item, including the name of the manufacturer and supplier

- The cost of the item

- Why you believe the purchase is necessary

- The impact of the items on the unit's or organization's operating revenues and expenses

Including a Contingency Line

It's a good idea to have a contingency line built into the capital budget for emergency items. The purpose of the contingency line is to cover items that absolutely must be purchased during the year but, for some reason, were not included in the capital budget (so-called surprise items). It's always better to ask to spend budgeted dollars than to request items that were not budgeted for!

When I was a chief nursing officer (CNO), the chief executive officer (CEO) taught me the importance of building a contingency line into the capital budget. He always built a contingency line of $250,000 for the entire hospital's capital budget. One year, the facility had to replace the CT scan tube twice, instead of the anticipated once—totaling $60,000 instead of $30,000. Obviously, the CEO looked much better in front of the board of directors when he explained that this expenditure was covered in the capital budget's contingency line.

Summary

This chapter covered the following:

- Capital budgets
- Major movable equipment
- Fixed assets
- Capital investments
- Long-term investments
- Capital assets
- Capital acquisitions
- Capital items
- Developing a contingency line in the capital budget

7

Budget Variances

In general terms, *variance analysis* refers to the comparison of a budgeted amount with the actual amount to identify fiscal variances. The purpose of variance analysis is to identify what has caused this fiscal variance. Armed with this knowledge, the nurse manager can take corrective action to prevent such occurrences in the future.

> **NOTE**
>
> *You can't undo what has already been done, but you can take corrective action to improve operational and fiscal performance going forward.*

Conducting a Variance Analysis

When conducting a variance analysis, you analyze three items:

- **Efficiency.** Efficiency is also known as the quantity or use variable. If a nurse manager budgets for X number of hours of care per day, but provides more hours of care than he or she budgeted, that manager will have a negative variance, because more care hours provided translates to more dollars spent on staffing. In this situation, the nurse manager would not have been efficient.

- **Volume.** Volume variances relate to the number of patients for whom care was provided. Generally, increased patient volume means both increased revenue and increased cost. To provide the same number of nursing hours per patient day when increased volume exists, a nurse manager would need more staff.

- **Cost.** Cost variances relate to how many dollars are spent to deliver care. If a nurse manager were to provide more hours of care than were budgeted, the additional staffing to provide that care would likely be paid in overtime, agency, or bonus dollars, resulting in a higher cost to deliver the care.

UNDERSTANDING BONUS DOLLARS

Bonus dollars are generally dollars that are paid to entice an employee to work extra. For example, part-time employees usually will not get overtime unless they have worked 40 hours in a given week. As a way to encourage part-time employees to work an extra shift, organizations may offer a bonus rate, which is a higher rate than the part-time hourly rate.

It is not a great cause of concern if the cost variance is due to higher volume. If efficiency and cost variances increase but volume decreases, however, it is a cause of concern for an organization.

Calculating Variances

Table 7.1 shows a sample budget report from a 1-month period.

TABLE 7.1
SAMPLE BUDGET REPORT

	Budget	Actual	Budget Variance
Patient days	425	499	74
Nursing care hours	1790	2290	500
Average hourly pay rate	$40/hour	$45/hour	$5/hour
Total payroll costs	$56,925	$86,795	$29,870

As you can readily see, this nursing unit's total payroll costs are $29,870 over the budgeted amount of $56,925. Let's analyze the three critical items—efficiency, volume, and cost—to determine whether this variance is a cause for concern.

Step 1: Calculating the Efficiency Variance

To calculate efficiency variance, you begin by determining the budgeted and actual hours per patient day (HPPD). To calculate HPPD, divide the nursing care hours by the patient days.

Nursing Care Hours ÷ Patient Days = HPPD

Calculating HPPD.

So, in this example (refer to Table 7.1), you calculate the budgeted HPPD as follows:

$$1790 \div 425 = 4.2$$

The budgeted HPPD is 4.2.

To obtain the actual HPPD in this example, you calculate the following:

$$2{,}290 \div 499 = 4.5$$

The actual HPPD is 4.5.

Next, you must determine the average extra nursing care hours by subtracting the budgeted HPPD from the actual HPPD.

Actual HPPD
– Budgeted HPPD
= Average Extra Nursing Care Hours

Calculating the average extra nursing care hours.

So, in this example, the average extra nursing care hours would be as follows:

$$4.5 - 4.2 = 0.3$$

The average extra nursing care hours is 0.3.

Then, determine the total number of extra nursing care hours by multiplying the average extra nursing care hours by the actual number of patient days.

Average Extra Nursing Care Hours
x Actual Patient Days
= Total Extra Nursing Care Hours

Calculating the total extra nursing care hours.

In this example, total extra nursing care hours would be as follows:

$$0.3 \times 499 = 149.70$$

The total extra nursing care hours is 149.7.

Finally, calculate the efficiency variance by multiplying the total extra nursing care hours by the budgeted hourly wage.

Total Extra Nursing Care Hours
x Budgeted Hourly Wage
= Efficiency Variance

Calculating the efficiency variance.

In this example, the efficiency variance is calculated as follows:

$$149.70 \times \$40 = \$5,988$$

The efficiency variance is $5,988.

Step 2: Calculating the Volume Variance

Calculating the volume variance involves a similar series of formulas. To start, calculate the number of extra patient days by subtracting the budgeted patient days from the actual patient days (refer to Table 7.1).

Actual Patient Days
– Budgeted Patient Days
= Extra Patient Days

Calculating the number of extra patient days.

In this example, the extra patient days are as follows:

$$499 - 425 = 74$$

The extra patient days are 74.

Next, multiply the extra patient days (74) by the budgeted HPPD. This yields the extra nursing care hours provided.

Extra Patient Days
x Budgeted HPPD
= Extra Nursing Care Hours Provided

Calculating the extra nursing care hours provided.

In this example, the extra nursing care hours provided are as follows:

$$74 \times 4.2 = 310.80$$

The extra nursing care hours provided are 310.80.

Finally, multiply the extra nursing care hours provided by the budgeted hourly pay rate to calculate the volume variance.

Extra Nursing Care Hours Provided
x Budgeted Hourly Pay Rate
= Volume Variance

Calculating the volume variance.

In this example, the volume variance is as follows:

$$310.80 \times \$40 = \$12,432$$

The volume variance is $12,432.

Step 3: Calculating the Cost Variance

Calculating the cost variance is quite simple. To begin, you subtract the budgeted average hourly pay rate from the actual average hourly pay rate. This yields the cost difference.

Actual Average Hourly Rate Paid
– Budgeted Average Hourly Rate Paid
= Cost Difference

Calculating the cost difference.

Note: If the budgeted hourly rate is less than the actual average hourly rate paid, the multiplication will produce a positive number. If the actual average hourly rate paid is less than the budgeted hourly rate paid, the multiplication will produce a negative number. In the example, the actual average hourly rate paid is more than the budgeted average hourly rate, so the multiplication will produce a positive number.

$45 Per Hour Actual Paid
– Budget of $40 Per Hour
= The Cost Difference of $5.00 Per Hour

Calculating the cost difference.

Next, calculate the cost variance by multiplying the cost difference by the actual hours worked.

Cost Difference
x Actual Hours Worked
= Cost Variance

Calculating the cost variance.

In this example, the cost variance is as follows:

$$\$5 \times 2{,}290 = \$11{,}450$$

The cost variance is $11,450.

Putting It All Together

As a final step, add these three variances—the efficiency, volume, and cost variances—together to calculate the total variance.

Efficiency Variance
+ Volume Variance
+ Cost Variance
= Total Variance

Calculating the total variance.

In this example, the total variance is as follows:

$$\$5{,}988 + \$12{,}432 + \$11{,}450 = \$29{,}870$$

The total variance is $29,870.

Notice that the total variance equals $29,870—the same amount as the total variance over budget cited in Table 7.1. The numbers in the variance analysis demonstrate that volume and cost were the primary variance drivers. The question becomes, was this over-budget amount justified?

> **NOTE**
>
> *Most new nurse managers would argue that this overage is justified simply because the number of patient days was up by 74, regardless of whether this in fact contributed to the overage. The reality is, however, that one must get a little scientific about the process and really analyze what happened. It is not good enough to simply go with one's gut response!*

Because increased volume is considered a positive development, that area need not be considered further. In contrast, efficiency and costs are something that the nurse manager can control. Therefore, these areas require further evaluation.

With respect to efficiency variance, nurse managers should consider the following:

- Can staffing be made more flexible based on actual volumes?

- Is the appropriate skill mix being utilized?

- How do internal reports compare to prior months? For example, is this nursing unit consistently running over budget? If prior reports demonstrate the same pattern, perhaps the budgeting was done incorrectly, and not enough care hours were budgeted for initially.

In addition, when assessing efficiency, nurse managers should benchmark against available data for similar units in similar healthcare organizations. Healthcare organizations must benchmark themselves against other like and unlike organizations for comparison purposes. In a similar type of organization, what are the nursing care hours per patient day? How does this organization compare to that organization? This information can assist the nurse manager in designing the budget for the following year.

BUDGETING AND STANDARDS OF CARE

Budgeting for nursing hours of care per patient certainly ties to the standards of care that a nursing unit wants to provide. One of the better indicators for nursing care hours per patient day is an acuity system. In the past many such systems were very

continues >

subjective in nature as charge nurses would fill
in the level of care that they thought each patient
required. Oftentimes patients were listed as high
acuity patients when in reality they were not. Today
acuity systems are computerized and more objective
in nature. The acuity of the patient then specifies
the number of nursing care hours per patient day.
Although markedly improved, these computerized
systems are not perfect and some healthcare
facilities elect not to utilize them.

The vast majority of hospitals, nursing homes, and
other health facilities belong to national and/or
statewide organizations that collect data about
nursing care hours per patient day. When I was a
chief nursing officer (CNO), my hospital was a
member of the New Jersey Hospital Association
(NJHA). The NJHA is an affiliate of the American
Hospital Association (AHA). The NJHA would
collect data through surveys of the New Jersey
hospitals. For example, the nursing care hours per
patient day for medical surgical units would be
collected and reported for each hospital. NJHA
would also analyze this data and report on the
average nursing care hours per patient day on
medical-surgical nursing units in New Jersey
hospitals. As a CNO in New Jersey, I would get
these reports, and then I could benchmark the
nursing care hours per patient day to those
reported through the NJHA data.

With cost variance, nurse managers should consider the
following:

- Have there been changes in wages that were not
budgeted?

- Is the appropriate staff skill mix being utilized?

- Has more costly labor—for example, pool, bonus, or agency labor—been used?

- Is there a need to fill existing vacancies?

From this, you should be able to see how changes can be made to improve efficiency and control costs.

NOTE

Calculating efficiency, volume, and cost variances can improve your ability to diagnose problems and identify corrective measures to improve performance.

Summary

This chapter covered the following:

- Variance analysis

- Quantity of use or efficiency variance

- Volume variance

- Cost variance

- Formulas for calculating variances

- Strategies that nurse managers can employ to correct budget variances

8

Budget Reports

Given today's economic constraints and the focus on cost-effectiveness, quality care, and all the other driving economic forces behind healthcare, understanding and, more importantly, using budgets for effective management of resources is critical. The budget needs to be a tool that managers use to take action.

For that to be possible, reports are necessary. Reports, which must be viewed in a timely manner, provide nurse managers with extremely valuable information. With reports, you can track patterns and trends and perform variance analyses. Armed with this information, you can take necessary corrective measures to improve performance in upcoming budget cycles.

Types of Budget Reports

There are many different types of budget reports. Some reports are generated annually, some are generated monthly, and some are generated biweekly.

Annual reports in a healthcare organization might include the following:

- **Personnel Budget Worksheet.** This worksheet lists personnel budget expense items. This is a tool utilized by nurse managers.

- **Supply and Expense Budget Worksheet.** This worksheet lists supplies and related expenses. This is a tool utilized by nurse managers.

- **Budget Distribution Report.** This budget report is distributed to respective responsibility center managers.

Monthly reports in a healthcare organization might include the following:

- **Actual to Budget Comparison.** In this report, actual expenses that occurred during the specified time period are compared to those budgeted expenses.

- **Cost Distribution.** This is also known as distribution cost. To define the term generically, it can be costs distributed across a product line in healthcare (for example, an orthopedic product line). Another way to view this is the total cost spent for goods or services, including money, time, and labor. In healthcare, you can look at how much cost is distributed over a lifetime. For example, data demonstrates that after the first year of life, healthcare costs are lowest for children, rise slowly throughout adult life, and increase significantly after the age of 50. Human resource management also distributes the cost of employees, which would include salary costs, health insurance costs, benefit costs, tuition reimbursement costs, and so on.

- **Inventory Monthly Distribution.** This is a monthly distribution report for inventory. This report is utilized to control inventory.

- **Payroll Position Control Listing.** The human resources department and nursing managers utilize this report. This report lists what employee positions have been filled and what vacancies exist. It is a report that helps nursing managers and HR directors avoid over hiring staff (that is, to not hire staff when all positions have already been filled).

Biweekly reports in a healthcare organization might include the following:

- **Detailed Departmental Summary.** Summarizes activities for a given time period for a nursing unit or department.

- **Employees Not Working Authorized Hours.** Employees who did not work scheduled hours. This results if an employee is on vacation, medical leave, or family medical leave of absence.

If your organization permits it, consider working with colleagues in the finance department to develop reports that are tailored to meet your specific needs.

A nurse manager may want a customized report so that he or she can better manage a budget. I found this necessary when I became a chief nursing officer (CNO). I met with the finance budget manager and advised him that if I were to better manage operations in my department I needed a report that I could understand and that made sense to me. He then met with me, and we discussed what I needed. For example, I wanted overtime hours broken out by skill mix, registered nurse (RN), licensed practical nurse (LPN), nursing assistant, and clerical. I also wanted a category for agency nursing and how many full-time employees (FTEs) that equated to. This provided me with much needed information so that I could better manage and control the budget.

FINANCIAL REPORTS

Financial reports identify revenue generated and expenses incurred over a period of time, generally for 1 calendar month or a 28-day time period. Such reports display the totals for the year to date for the unit, department, and organization. Items are sorted into groups and reported by accounts. Expenses are generally sorted into employment costs and non-salary expenses. These reports typically show the actual and budgeted revenues and expenses for the month and year to date, as well as any variances.

Example 1: Comparative Staff Summary Report 1

Let's look at some examples of reports, starting with the Comparative Staff Summary Report shown in Figure 8.1. This report is detailed for pay period 16 at Hospital X. In this organization, pay periods run biweekly.

This report details the following:

- The budget for this pay period
- The actual dollar amount for this pay period
- The year-to-date performance (i.e., what has actually occurred during the first 16 pay periods)

PAY PERIOD 16
NURSING STATION:3RD

CSSPRT
PROCESS DATE:8/03/15

STATISTICAL DATA	2015 BUDGET	2015 ACTUAL PAY PERIOD 16	2015 ACTUAL YTD PAY PERIOD 16
BEDS IN SERVICE	39	39	39
ADMISSIONS	55	52	810
PATIENT DAYS	519	479	8,123
LENGTH OF STAY	9.4	9.2	10
AVERAGE DAILY CENSUS	37	34	36
PERCENT OCCUPANCY %	95.1	87.7	93
FTE (STAFFED)	33	37.1	35.8
HOURS (STAFFED)	2,641.0	2,965.2	45,918.5
HOURS/PATIENT DAY	5.1	6.2	5.7

FIGURE 8.1
Comparative Staff Summary Report 1.

When analyzing this report, you can see the following:

- The budgeted hours of care per patient day were 5.1 hours. During the 16th pay period, however, the unit actually delivered 6.2 hours of care per patient day. Thus, this nursing unit was over by 1.1 care hours per patient day. (You might say to yourself, "No big deal." But if every nursing unit were over by that number of care hours, there would be severe financial consequences to the organization.)

To review, you calculate the actual nursing care hours (here, 6.2 per patient per day) by dividing the hours staffed (here, 2,965.2) by the patient days (in this report, 479).

- Year to date (YTD), the care hours are 5.7. So, overall, the unit is 0.6 care hours over budget. If the trend of delivering more care hours on a biweekly basis continues, however, the YTD hours could be significantly over budget by year's end.

The appropriate thing to do here is to conduct a variance analysis to see what is causing the over-budget situation, although you can garner a lot from the report itself. Specifically, according to the report, both admissions and patient days are down. There were 55 admissions budgeted, but only 52 actual admissions for this pay period. In addition, although there were 519 patient days budgeted, there were only 479 actual patient days for this time period. This is most likely driving the over-budget situation.

Example 2: Comparative Staff Summary Report 2

The Comparative Staff Summary Report shown in Figure 8.2 reveals considerable historical data, including the following:

- Beds in service
- Admissions

- Patient days
- Length of stay
- Average daily census
- Percent occupancy
- FTE (staffed)
- Hours (staffed)
- Hours/patient day

PAY PERIOD 16
NURSING STATION: 3RD
COMPARATIVE STAFFING SUMMARY

STATISTICAL DATA	2012 ACTUAL	2013 ACTUAL	2014 ACTUAL	2015 ACTUAL
BEDS IN SERVICE	39	39	39	39
ADMISSIONS	1,158	1,158	1,259	1,359
PATIENT DAYS	13,392	13,647	13,749	12,807
LENGTH OF STAY	11.6	11.8	10.9	9.4
AVERAGE DAILY CENSUS	37	37	38	35
PERCENT OCCUPANCY %	94.1	95.9	96.6	90.0
FTE (STAFFED)	34.9	35.4	36.6	35.5
HOURS (STAFFED)	72,482	73,641	76,022	73,913
HOURS/PATIENT DAY	5.7	5.4	5.5	5.8

FIGURE 8.2
Comparative Staff Summary Report 2.

This report not only provides information about current operations, but it also serves as a great tool for planning services and budgets in the future. For example, through 2013, the average daily census and patient days were increasing. If that trend were to continue, you would likely need to increase staffing levels in future budgets to deliver the budgeted nursing care hours.

Notice that this report calculates the average length of stay. This is the first time that this formula is discussed. To calculate the average length of stay, you divide the total patient days for the given period by the total number of admissions during that same period.

Patient Days in a Given Period ÷ Number of Admissions During That Period = Average Length of Stay

Calculating the average length of stay.

For example, the average length of stay in 2014 was as follows:

12,807 ÷ 1,359 = 9.4

The average length of stay in 2014 was 9.4 days.

Example 3: Comparative Staff Summary Report 3

The Comparative Staff Summary Report shown in Figure 8.3 details the levels of staffing based on skill level used in this particular nursing unit. A comparison is made between budgeted and actual staffing for pay period 16.

Highlights of the report include the following:

- This report shows that 0.1 hour is budgeted for the department head or supervisor, who is listed separately. In a 2-week period, this would equate to 4 hours of care being provided by the department head. The report correctly does not count the administrative functions of this job toward the hours per patient day.

- This unit used no agency staff during this period.

- Roughly 60% of the care on this unit is provided by registered nurses. This unit also utilizes LPNs, nursing aides, clerical staff, and orderlies.

- The actual care hours provided exceed the budgeted care hours provided. The FTEs also are over budget for this period.

- Overtime hours are below budget for this period.

- The actual productive hours per patient day (PRD HR/PAT DAY) was over budget for this period.

Example 4: Comparative Staffing Report 4

The Comparative Staffing Report shown in Figure 8.4 is identical to the Comparative Staffing Report shown in Figure 8.3, except in this report, the comparisons are for the YTD actual for the 16 pay periods.

STAFFING DATA	PAY PERIOD BUDGET						PAY PERIOD 16					
SKILL LEVEL	FTE	TOTAL HOURS	OT	OTHER	PROD. HOURS	PRD HR/ PAT DAY	FTE	TOTAL HOURS	OT	OTHER	PROD. HOURS	PRD HR/ PAT DAY
.01 RN'S & GN'S	14.4	1149	21	1013	1034	2	20.5	1642.2	25.2	1545.5	1570.7	3.3
.02 LPN'S	11.9	955	12	848	860	1.7	9.9	789.2	10	749.8	759.8	1.6
.03 AIDES	2.7	216	8	186	194	0.4	1.5	120.0	0.0	111.0	111.0	0.2
.08 SUPR & DEPT HEADS	1.0	80	0	72	72	0.1	1	80	0.0	80	80	0.2
AGENCY	0.0	0	0	0	0	0.0	0.0	0.0	0.0	0.0	0.0	0.0
SUBTOTAL	30	2400	41	2119	2160	4.2	32.9	2631.4	35.2	2486.3	2521.5	5.3
.04 TECHNICIANS	0	0	0	0	0	0	0.0	0.0	0.0	0.0	0.0	0.0
.05 CLERICAL	2	160	8	136	144	0.3	3.2	253.8	2.9	205.2	208.1	0.4
.07 OTHER PROFESSIONALS	0	0	0	0	0	0	0.0	0.0	0.0	0.0	0.0	0.0
.09 ORDERLIES	1	81	2	71	73	0.1	1.0	80.0	0.0	80.0	80.0	0.2
TOTAL	33	2641	51	2326	2377	4.6	37.1	2965.2	38.1	2771.5	2809.6	5.9

CALCULATED FTES: 37.1

FIGURE 8.3
Comparative Staff Summary Report 3.

STAFFING DATA

SKILL LEVEL	FTE	TOTAL HOURS	OT	OTHER	PROD. HOURS	PRD HR/ PAT DAY
.01 RN'S & GN'S	16.5	21147.7	550.5	19116.2	19666.7	2.4
.02 LPN'S	12.6	16083.3	486.2	13916.5	14402.7	1.8
.03 AIDES	2.2	2778.3	68.5	2469.3	2537.8	0.3
.08 SUPR & DEPT HEADS	0.8	1064.1	0	1025.7	1025.7	0.1
AGENCY	0.0	0	0	0	0	0.0
SUBTOTAL	**32.1**	**41073.4**	**1105.2**	**36527.7**	**37632.9**	**4.6**
.04 TECHNICIANS	0	0	0	0	0	0
.05 CLERICAL	3	3889.6	18.4	3483.7	3502.1	0.4
.07 OTHER PROFESSIONALS	0	0	0	0	0	0
.09 ORDERLIES	0.7	955.5	11.9	832.5	844.4	0.1
TOTAL	**35.8**	**45918.5**	**1135.5**	**40843.9**	**41979.4**	**5.1**

YTD PAY PERIOD

CALCULATED FTES: 35.8

FIGURE 8.4

Comparative Staff Summary Report 4.

Example 5: Comparative Staffing Report for the ICU/CCU

This report, shown in Figure 8.5, is a combination of the preceding four reports. It puts everything together. In it, you can view the historical data and all the other items discussed in the first four comparative staffing reports.

The chief nursing officer in an organization might obtain such a report for each nursing unit and an overall summary report for the entire nursing division. Ideally, these reports would run every 2 weeks, when the biweekly payroll cycle runs. This would provide timely information, enabling nurse managers to take action to avoid overspending during the next 2-week period.

Example 6: Staff Mix Analysis Report

This report, shown in Figure 8.6, demonstrates the breakdown of actual care hours by skill level—for example, registered nurse (RN), graduate nurse (GN), licensed practical nurse (LPN), licensed graduate practical nurse (LGPN), nursing assistant, and orderly—compared to the standard care hours budgeted for this unit.

PAY PERIOD 15
NURSING STATION: ICU/CCU

CSSRPT
PROCESS DATE: 7/22/15
TIME: 11:31:03

COMPARATIVE STAFFING SUMMARY

STATISTICAL DATA	2013 ACTUAL	2014 ACTUAL	2015 BUDGET	2015 ACTUAL PAY PERIOD 15	2015 ACTUAL YTD PAY PERIOD 15
BEDS IN SERVICE	13	12	13	13	13
ADMISSIONS	497	446	20	10	175
PATIENT DAYS	4,042	4,099	150	176	2572
LENGTH OF STAY	8.1	9.2	7.5	17.6	14.7
AVERAGE DAILY CENSUS	11	11	11	13	12
PERCENT OCCUPANCY %	85.2	93.6	82.4	96.7	94.2
FTE (STAFFED)	35.7	41.3	44.8	43.3	42.7
FTE (AGENCY)	3.2	1	0	0	0
HOURS (STAFFED)	74,308	85,815	3,586	3,468.2	51,210.6
HOURS (AGENCY)	6,713	2,161	0	0	0
HOURS/PATIENT DAY	20.0	21.5	23.9	19.7	19.9

FIGURE 8.5
Comparative Staffing Report for the ICU/CCU.

FIGURE 8.5, CONTINUED
Comparative Staffing Report for the ICU/CCU.

STAFFING DATA

SKILL LEVEL	PAY PERIOD 15						YTD PAY PERIOD					
	FTE	TOTAL HOURS	OT	OTHER	PROD HOURS	PRD HR/ PAT DAY	FTE	TOTAL HOURS	OT	OTHER	PROD HOURS	PRD HR/ PAT DAY
.01 RN'S & GN'S	35.9	2873.4	243.0	2322.4	2565.4	14.6	34.1	40878.0	4110.2	33081.5	37191.7	14.5
.02 LPN'S	4.0	322.0	17.0	269.0	286.0	1.6	4.0	4818.9	513.8	3401.9	3924.7	1.5
.03 AIDES	1.0	82.2	2.2	80.0	82.0	0.5	1.0	1214.6	9.4	1078.3	1087.7	.4
.08 SUPR & DEPT HEADS	1.0	80.0	.0	79.5	79.5	0.5	1.9	2246.9	.0	2013.8	2013.8	.8
AGENCY	.0	.0	.0	.0	.0	.0	.0	.0	.0	.0	.0	.0
SUBTOTAL	**41.9**	**3357.6**	**262.2**	**2750.9**	**3013.1**	**17.2**	**41.0**	**49158.4**	**4633.4**	**39584.5**	**44217.9**	**17.2**
.04 TECHNICIANS	.0	.0	.0	.0	.0	.0	.1	104.0	8.0	96.0	104.0	.0
.05 CLERICAL	1.4	110.6	14.6	96.0	110.6	.6	1.5	1776.9	221.0	1501.4	1722.4	.7
.07 OTHER PROFESSIONALS	.0	.0	.0	.0	.0	.0	.0	12.0	.0	12.0	12.0	.0
.09 ORDERLIES	.0	.0	.0	.0	.0	.0	.1	159.3	7.0	152.3	159.3	.1
TOTAL	**43.3**	**3468.2**	**276.8**	**2846.9**	**3123.7**	**17.8**	**42.7**	**51210.6**	**4869.4**	**41346.2**	**46215.6**	**18.0**

CALCULATED FTES: 43.4

CALCULATED FTES: 42.7

Example 7: Nursing Care Hour Report

Someone once said that a picture is worth a thousand words. This is especially true of graphs, like the one contained in the Nursing Care Hour Report shown in Figure 8.7. This report contains a nice graph that compares actual hours delivered to the standard budgeted hours. This enables nurse managers to see at a glance whether they are in line with the budget, over budget, or under budget.

Summary

This chapter discussed the following:

- The various types of budget reports
- Sample Excel worksheets containing budgets

DATE:
ACTUAL vs STANDARD NURSING CARE HOURS

SHIFT STANDARD N.C.H.						ACTUAL NURSING CARE HOURS				
	OB	PEDS	2H	3H	4H	5H	5S	5W	DETOX
7a–3p	2.0	2.1	7.2	1.6	1.9	3.1	1.9	2.0	4.0	1.0
3p–11p	1.5	-	-	1.4	2.1	1.8	1.5	1.6	4.0	1.8
11p–7a	1.0	3.5	8.0	1.0	1.1	1.5	1.0	1.2	4.0	2.0
TOTAL:	4.5	5.6	15.2	4.0	5.1	6.4	4.4	4.8	12.0	4.8

	ICU/CCU			PICU	
SHIFT	S.N.C.H.	A.N.C.H.	SHIFT	S.N.C.H.	A.N.C.H.
7a-7p	7.5	8.3	7a-7p	3.75	4.2
7p-7a	7.5	10.2	7p-7a	3.75	2.9
TOTAL:	15.0	18.5	TOTAL:	7.5	7.1

STAFF MIX ANALYSIS ICU/CCU, PICU

		RN	GN	LPN	ASST'S & AIDES	ORT'S
ICU/CCU	7a-7p	8	~	~	~	1
	7p-7a	6	~	2	~	3
PICU	7a-7p	3	~	3	~	1
	7p-7a	4	~	1	~	~

STAFF MIX ANALYSIS

		OB	PEDS	2H	3H	4H	5H	5S	5W	DETOX
RN	7a-3p	7	2	2	2	2	3	4	1	1
	3p-11p	~	~	3	3	3	3	4	1	2
	11p-7a	6	1	2	3	3	1	3	1	1
GN	7a-3p	~	~	2	~	~	~	~	~	~
	3p-11p	~	~	0.5	1	~	1	~	~	~
	11p-7a	~	~	2	~	~	~	~	~	~
LPN	7a-3p	1	1	1	5	2	3	2	1	1
	3p-11p	~	~	2	2.5	1	1	3	~	1
	11p-7a	2	1	1	1	1	3	2	~	1
GPN	7a-3p	~	~	~	~	~	~	~	~	~
	3p-11p	~	~	~	~	~	~	~	~	~
	11p-7a	~	~	~	~	~	~	~	~	~
ASST'S & AIDES	7a-3p	~	~	2	2	3	1	2	~	~
	3p-11p	~	~	1	1	2	1	~	~	~
	11p-7a	1	~	~	1	1	~	~	~	~
ORT'S	7a-3p	~	~	~	~	3	1	2	~	~
	3p-11p	~	~	~	1	~	~	1	~	~
	11p-7a	1	~	~	~	~	~	1	~	~

S.N.C.H. = Standard Nursing Care Hours   ANCH = staff x hours   A.N.C.H. = Actual Nursing Care Hours

FIGURE 8.6
Staff Mix Analysis Report.

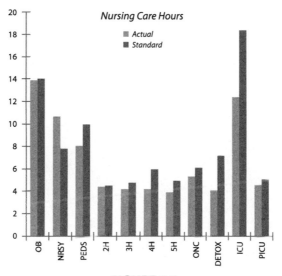

FIGURE 8.7
Nursing Care Hour Report.

9

Healthcare Reform and the Affordable Care Act

The United States has an entrepreneurial healthcare system, with a variety of products in the marketplace. When you contrast the U.S. healthcare delivery system with that of other countries, it is rather clear that huge costs are attributable to administrative functions. Countries with less variety of insurance products tend to have much lower overhead when compared to the United States.

This traditional U.S. health insurance market worked well for the insurance industry, but not so well for many patients and clinicians. For example, in 2013 an estimated 42+ million Americans were uninsured, with tens of millions more being underinsured, and those with coverage were often afraid of losing it (Smith & Medal, 2013). Many medical practices lacked the support that they needed to provide coordinated, safe, effective, outcome-oriented, patient-centered care.

Why Reform?

Arguably (and the debate about reform did result in many arguments), the U.S. healthcare system was broken and needed to be repaired. Essential care providers faced crushing paperwork, uncertainty regarding payment, and rising healthcare costs. The insurance bureaucracy was adding more paperwork to medical practices, which reduced their time spent with patients. Patients with no coverage or limited coverage would often forgo or delay seeking needed care and treatment. This resulted in patients presenting to emergency departments very ill and thus requiring costly treatment. Healthcare outcomes in the United States continued to lag behind many other countries despite spending far more on care.

Two of the leading indicators that assess a country's healthcare system are life expectancy and infant mortality. In the year 2000, the last year that the World Health Organization assessed all countries' healthcare delivery systems, the United States ranked 37th out of 191 countries analyzed. The United States was considered an intervention system. Also, other countries' health systems ranked higher than the United States regarding good primary care systems that were lacking in the United States. In short, the U.S. healthcare system needed a major overhaul.

According to the Organisation for Economic Co-operation and Development (OECD; 2015), life expectancy in the United States has increased since 1970. However, it has grown at a much slower rate compared to other nations. The OECD contributes this to poor health-related behaviors in the United States and the fragmentation of our healthcare delivery system.

What is meant by saying the United States is an intervention system? To better explain what this is you need to take a look at many United States citizen behaviors. A vast majority of Americans feel that they can a take a pill and make it all better. My mom once told me a story that I tell a lot. She was watching a television show with two police officers. They went to each lunch, and one of the officers ordered a large juicy cheeseburger with all of the toppings. The other officer commented to his partner that he thought his partner had hyperlipidemia and needed to watch his cholesterol intake. The officer about to consume this large cheeseburger immediately took out a Lipitor tablet. He put the tablet in the center of the cheeseburger and then ate it and stated that now he took care of his ingestion of too much cholesterol. The point of the story is that health behaviors would have people eating proper diets and exercising so that medication would not be necessary to treat something.

The United States is wonderful with creating and utilizing technology. There is no question that I like to be near an American hospital when I travel. The technology, however good it may be, also brings interventions. Again, the attitude of some Americans is that one can correct any condition with either a medication, a procedure, or surgery when in reality a lot of what needs correcting could have been prevented through healthy behaviors and lifestyle modifications.

Finally, there is a definite correlation between primary care and healthy behaviors. Primary care providers provide health promotion. They discuss with patients diet, exercise, smoking cessation, etc. They monitor patient cholesterol, blood pressure, heart rate, and other parameters, so that if something is abnormal or is starting to elevate, for example, cholesterol level, they can recommend treatments as well as healthy behaviors in order to prevent costly interventions. Countries that have better health indicators than the United States usually have better primary care systems as opposed to hospitals and intervention systems of care.

PERSONAL HEALTHCARE IMPACTS

There was a family friend of mine. Let's call him Kurt. At age 15 Kurt developed a gynecomastia (male breast enlargement). His right breast had become so large that Kurt would no longer participate in physical education at his school because his classmates were making fun of him in the locker room when they saw his chest. His mother came to me because she knew I was in healthcare and was the chief nursing officer (CNO) at the hospital. She told me that they did not have healthcare insurance and, as such, could not get Kurt surgery, which was required to correct the gynecomastia. I was able to get her help. I contacted our finance office who was able to help them with applying for charity care funding in our state. Once the funding was approved, Kurt was able to have his surgical procedure.

And here is my own story. I was married and our 3-month-old son was diagnosed with a right indirect inguinal hernia, a congenital birth defect. Our family physician referred us to a surgeon. I had just started working as an orderly in an operating room, my first job in a hospital. It was my first week of employment when my son was diagnosed. We did not have healthcare insurance. My mom went to the family doctor with my wife. She asked whether he could refer us to a surgeon where I was now working. Our family physician complied with my mom's request. I had literally met this surgeon one time in the operating room since I had been employed there that week. Both the surgeon and the anesthesiologist did not charge us for their services since I was employed at the hospital. I could not believe what they had done for us. After all, I was

> at that hospital in that operating room for less than a week. It restored my faith in humanity and also demonstrated to me that there are indeed a lot of caring physicians out there.

As you learned in Chapter 2, the United States has contemplated healthcare reform many times over many years. Figure 9.1 briefly describes healthcare reform history in the United States.

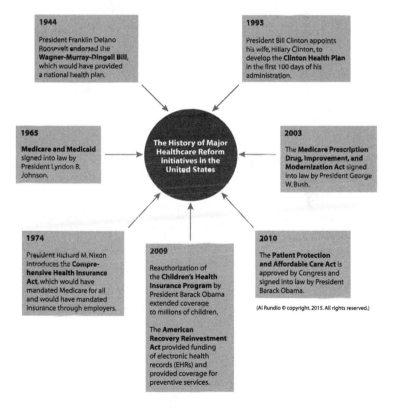

1944

President Franklin Delano Roosevelt endorsed the **Wagner-Murray-Dingell Bill**, which would have provided a national health plan.

1993

President Bill Clinton appoints his wife, Hillary Clinton, to develop the **Clinton Health Plan** in the first 100 days of his administration.

1965

Medicare and Medicaid signed into law by President Lyndon B. Johnson.

The History of Major Healthcare Reform Initiatives in the United States

2003

The **Medicare Prescription Drug, Improvement, and Modernization Act** signed into law by President George W. Bush.

1974

President Richard M. Nixon introduces the **Comprehensive Health Insurance Act**, which would have mandated Medicare for all and would have mandated insurance through employers.

2009

Reauthorization of the **Children's Health Insurance Program** by President Barack Obama extended coverage to millions of children.

The **American Recovery Reinvestment Act** provided funding of electronic health records (EHRs) and provided coverage for preventive services.

2010

The **Patient Protection and Affordable Care Act** is approved by Congress and signed into law by President Barack Obama.

FIGURE 9.1
Healthcare Reform History in the United States.

The Affordable Care Act

Landmark healthcare reform legislation, the Patient Protection and Affordable Care Act (ACA), was finally passed under the Obama administration in March 2010 to address the issues discussed earlier in this chapter. The Patient Protection and Affordable Care Act was determined, after multiple challenges at various judicial levels, to be constitutional in 2012 by the U.S. Supreme Court with the exception of forcing states to expand Medicaid.

The overriding themes of the ACA include the following:

- Access to care by expanding Medicaid and insurance coverage through healthcare insurance exchanges.

- Cost control by the creation of accountable care organizations with bundled billing and payments and other innovations.

- Quality improvement to lower costs through reductions in hospital-acquired infections (nosocomial infections), electronic health records, and the measurement of outcomes.

- Increased revenue through taxes on medical devices, pharmaceutical companies, cosmetic surgery, and tanning salons (and a reduction in flexible spending accounts).

- Financial support for nursing schools and changes to loan-forgiveness programs for physicians entering the National Health Service Corps. Innovation awards are built in to the act.

- Creating transparency between pharmaceutical companies, physicians, healthcare providers, and others.

Figure 9.2 graphically shows some of the key benefits of the ACA.

Benefits for Women
Providing insurance options, covering preventive services, and lowering costs.

Young Adult Coverage
Coverage available to children up to age 26.

Strengthening Medicare
Yearly wellness visit and many free preventive services for some seniors with Medicare.

Holding Insurance Companies Accountable
Insurers must justify any premium increase of 10% or more before the rate takes effect.

FIGURE 9.2
Benefits of the ACA
(Graphic provided by U.S. Department of Health & Human Services 2015)

Key Provisions

Key provisions of the ACA include the following:

- New protections that hold insurers accountable

- Expanded insurance coverage to more than 34 million people

> **NOTE**
>
> *The reasons why people have been unable to obtain insurance are varied:*
>
> - *Cost of insurance is too high for some individuals*
> - *Many do not have access to insurance coverage through a job*
> - *In states that did not expand Medicaid many such*

continues >

> *individuals are ineligible for public insurance coverage*
> * *Illegal or undocumented immigrants are ineligible for Medicaid or Marketplace insurance coverage (The Henry J. Kaiser Family Foundation, 2015).*

* Reduction in administrative burden so that clinicians can spend more time with their patients

* New models of care that create more opportunities to coordinate care across the continuum, such as an accountable care organization

* New protections that strengthen patient coverage, a medical practice, and the entire healthcare delivery system

* Medicaid expansion

* Bans on:

  * Preexisting condition exclusions

  * Annual and lifetime caps on benefits

* Coverage for young adults up to age 26 on their parent's insurance plan

* More plan choices

* Cadillac tax effective 2018

NOTE

The Cadillac tax refers to a 40% tax on the cost of healthcare coverage that exceeds predetermined threshold dollar amounts for high-cost, employer-sponsored healthcare coverage. If the employer carries insurance, the tax is paid by the insurer. If the employer uses self-funded plans, the payment is made by the employer. The Cadillac tax is not deductible for federal income tax purposes.

* Preventive services covered without out-of-pocket

copayments

- New models of care, such as accountable care organizations and medical homes

- Value-based purchasing

- Bundled payments

- Electronic health records

- Patient-Centered Outcomes Research Institute

> **NOTE**
>
> The Patient-Centered Outcomes Research Institute (PCORI) is an independent nonprofit, nongovernmental organization located in Washington, DC. This institute was authorized by Congress in 2010.
>
> The mandate of PCORI is to improve the quality and relevance of evidence available to help patients, caregivers, clinicians, employers, insurers, and policy makers make informed health decisions.
>
> This organization funds comparative clinical effectiveness research (CER), as well as supports work that will improve the methods used to conduct such studies.
>
> You can find more information about PCORI at http://www.pcori.org/about-us

- Simplification of paperwork through electronic health records

- States allowed to offer their own healthcare insurance plans

New Protections

The ACA ensures fair treatment for patients and providers. New protections will end the worst insurance industry excesses and abuses in the system, such as the following:

- The law will prevent denials of coverage for

preexisting conditions.

- Insurance companies cannot cancel coverage because patients made a mistake on their insurance coverage application.

- Gender equality will be ensured because insurance companies will not be able to charge women more than men.

- The ACA eliminates lifetime benefit limits and phases out annual limits.

In addition, post-ACA, insurance companies are required to spend 80% to 85% of premium dollars on direct patient care. Before the ACA, insurance companies spent as much as 40% of every premium dollar on overhead, marketing, and chief executive officer salaries. After passage of the ACA, insurance companies must now spend at least 80% of every premium dollar on consumer healthcare. Should they not spend this amount, they must then repay the shortfall to those paying the premiums.

Under the ACA, insurers can no longer exclude coverage based on preexisting conditions. In addition, the vast majority of young adults who are not attending college can remain on their parents' health plans until the age of 26. This mandate became effective with implementation of the ACA in 2010, but coverage only applies to medical care. The act does not mandate insuring young adults for dental or vision care.

NOTE

Preexisting condition insurance plans, known as PCIP plans, are now available. These plans exist in every state for people who have been locked out of the insurance market because of a preexisting condition such as cancer or heart disease. For more information, visit www.PCIP.gov.

Affordability

The ACA makes healthcare insurance more affordable through state health insurance exchanges, premium tax credits, and subsidies. The act reduces the burden of uncompensated care on physicians and hospitals, and also provides tax credits for small businesses.

Under the ACA, the minimum essential health benefits for all persons insured in the United States include the following:

- Ambulatory patient services

- Prescription pharmaceuticals

- Access to emergency services

- Inpatient hospitalization

- Maternity and newborn care

- Rehabilitative services and devices

- Laboratory services

- Mental health and substance-use-disorder care

- Pediatric services, inclusive of oral and vision care

The ACA also strengthens the Medicare system. It preserves guaranteed benefits under Medicare. The ACA makes recommended preventive services available without cost-sharing. It provides patients with an annual wellness visit. The ACA reduces cost-sharing across the board. It provides a 50% discount on covered brand-name drugs in the prescription drug doughnut hole (which resulted in an average savings of nearly $600 per person back in 2011). The ACA gradually closes the doughnut hole by the year 2020. The ACA also includes strong antifraud measures for Medicare recipients, including tougher penalties for criminals.

Additional Benefits

Other provisions of the ACA include investment in the training of new healthcare providers and providing bonus payments to primary care providers, which should add thousands of new doctors and nurses around the country. The ACA reduces administrative burdens. It creates new rules that standardize and simplify the claims and payment processes. This should result in fewer phone calls to patients and plans and should also reduce postage and paperwork cost. The ACA fully supports the use of electronic health records and invests in programs designed to help practices transition to electronic payment and record systems. All of this should result in the provider being able to spend more time in the exam room with the patient and less time on administrative tasks.

Other benefits created by the ACA include Medicare bonus payments for primary care physicians and general surgeons. It will also increase Medicaid primary care payments. The ACA increases geographic adjustments to Medicare physician payments in 42 states and territories. It also provides small-business tax credits for employee health insurance, which many practices may be eligible for. It also streamlines claims processing requirements in an attempt to decrease administrative costs. The ACA builds on best practices of physicians and medical groups across the country. It includes provisions for developing and implementing important payment and delivery system reforms that focus on expanding team-based care coordination, rewarding clinicians for care outside of traditional face-to-face visits, focusing on aggressive management of chronically ill patients, expanding access to home-based care, and ensuring that clinicians have seamless, secure ways to share patient information and medical records.

Electronic Health Records

The ACA invests in electronic health records. The Recovery Act created financial incentives for providers who adopt electronic health records. More than 176,049 providers registered for the Medicare and Medicaid electronic health record incentive programs. More than $2.5 billion has already been paid out in incentive payments. Electronic health record technology creates better coordinated and more efficient care, which leads to safer and higher quality patient care by reducing medical errors, by reducing redundant testing procedures, by having better availability of records and data, by improved clinical decision support systems for providers, and by improving safety and convenience of electronic prescribing. Electronic prescribing eliminates handwritten prescriptions, which will improve quality through more legible prescriptions. Easier and secure access to the patient's medical history will assist providers in making better treatment decisions.

Accountable Care Organizations

Accountable care organizations are a significant concept in the ACA. Such programs create partnerships for patients. The accountable care organization consists of a medical home, which is either primary care or a clinic. The purpose of the medical home is to coordinate care across the continuum and across services. Just as the name implies, accountable care organizations are "accountable" for the quality and cost-effectiveness of the care provided. Value-based purchasing is a critical component of an accountable care organization.

Accountable care organizations consist of many types of providers, such as primary care, acute care, psychiatric/mental healthcare, rehabilitation care, and home care. New models of care and payment systems to support Medicare and Medicaid enrollees will be explored. New models of care that incorporate behavioral health into the primary care setting will be trialed. Comprehensive primary care initiatives and federally qualified health centers with advanced primary care practice demonstration projects will be initiated. Healthcare innovation challenges and innovation advisors programs to look at innovative models of care delivery will be implemented.

> **NOTE**
>
> *Value-based purchasing is a strategy to measure, report, and reward quality and excellence in healthcare delivery.*
>
> *Hospital Value-Based Purchasing (VBP) is part of the Centers for Medicare & Medicaid Services (CMS) strategy to link Medicare's payment system to a value-based system. This system rewards hospitals that improve healthcare quality. (CMS, 2015)*

Impact and Future Trends

Healthcare in the United States under the ACA is likely to change in a number of ways in the future, including the following:

- Integrated delivery systems of care
- A shift from inpatient intervention care to primary preventive care
- Providers changing their focus by keeping indivduals healthy and out of emergency departments and hospitals
- Digital and electronic medicine and nursing
- Telemedicine, telehealth, and telenursing
- Hospital mergers and closures (see the following section)
- A decrease in employer-paid healthcare

- A decrease in healthcare inflation
- Innovative changes to medical and nursing school curriculum
- Innovative and new models of care delivery
- Strategic partnering (see the following section)

It is important for nurse managers to understand the impact on healthcare that the Patient Protection and Affordable Care Act of 2010 is having on hospitals and other healthcare providers. The vast majority of changes started in 2014. The reality is that reimbursement will change. There will be a much greater emphasis on preventive and primary care services and health promotion. Population health and keeping individuals healthy and out of the hospital will become the norm. The impact will be care delivery in a variety of settings. The acutely ill will be in the hospital. A renewed emphasis on quality and tying payment to quality care outcomes will become more and more important. In order to better prepare and understand budgets nurse managers need to fully understand the major implications of this act.

Hospital Mergers, Closures, and Strategic Partnering

In many states, hospitals have begun to merge into larger health systems, resulting in the subsequent closure of some hospitals. I have spoken anecdotally with colleagues who doubt that a single hospital will survive in the near future. Some predict that there will instead be 100 to 200 large regional health systems. Some predict fewer and larger national health systems; for example, every hospital will be part of one of 8 to 10 national systems. And some independent hospitals feel that they will survive as stand-alone facilities.

I always view the state that I reside in as a microcosm of what may occur. New Jersey is a very densely populated state that encompasses both urban and rural environments. It is sandwiched in the northeast corridor with easy access to major cities like Philadelphia, New York, Baltimore, Washington, D.C., and Boston. It is located in one of the busiest areas in the country, so I believe that it is a good representation of what may come in the future.

New Jersey is seeing both the mergers in healthcare systems (for example, two hospital systems coming together as one, smaller health system with three or four hospitals) and some stand-alone hospitals are still surviving. What definitely is occuring in almost all of these types of delivery systems is the practice known as strategic partnering. Strategic partnering refers to partnering with other types of facilities, not necessarily healthcare facilities, to achieve economy of scale and to maximize talent. One example is a hospital system partnering with a university. Certain services like dietary could be shared between both organizations. The university could bring additional talent to the hospital system, and the hospital could serve as the major clinical site for the education of physicians, nurses, and other healthcare providers.

Another trend is that hospitals and hospital systems are going out of the walls of the hospital and are focusing on population health. For example, one health system has more than 60 outpatient facilities in various communities, such as the following:

- Urgent care centers
- Convenient care centers in places like shopping centers, stores, and pharmacies
- Health and wellness centers
- Radiology and laboratory centers
- Home health agencies

Trends are also changing in that potential customers will select a hospital based on the care provided and how their experience was in the urgent care center (using critera such as friendliness and competency of the staff who provided the care).

The reality is that healthcare and healthcare delivery systems are changing, and the changing reimbursement and finance is one of the major catalysts for this change. You, as nurse managers and future nurse managers, need to be aware of this changing financial landscape so you can be better prepared to develop, implement and monitor budgets, allocate resources to your staff and assure quality patient care with excellent outcomes. Nurses and nurse managers are in a pivotal position to be key stakeholders and change agents in an evolving healthcare delivery system.

Global Caps: The Future of Healthcare?

Massachusetts proposed legislation in 2012 that would establish a global cap on healthcare costs (Kliff, 2012). (The Massachusetts healthcare system served as a model for the ACA.) Such global caps can be established in a variety of ways. One way is to average the cost of healthcare expenditures by participant and then cap that amount to be spent each year.

For example, if I spend $5,000 on average per year on my healthcare, that is my cap limit, and I should be expected to have healthcare rendered to me annually not exceeding that capped dollar amount. The difficulty is that should I have a myocardial infarction in a given year and require bypass surgery, my healthcare costs may exceed $250,000 that year. Global caps can be placed on hospitals and insurance companies and other third-party payers with the goal of not having healthcare expenditures exceed the established global cap.

Some believe that global caps will help to control healthcare costs. Others think that some patients will not get the required treatment because both the hospital and insurance companies will deny some services to stay within the global capped amount. Others argue that until consumers really get more involved and accountable for their health, healthcare costs will be difficult to control.

Capitation is a precursor to global caps, and some consider capitation a form of global caps. With capitation, there is one fee per member per month paid to the provider regardless of how often the patient accesses or does not access health services.

One has to have a crystal ball to predict what will occur next in healthcare. What is certain is that the focus on controlling and reducing costs while improving quality and outcomes is here to stay.

Summary

This chapter discussed the following:

- Healthcare reform
- The Patient Protection and Affordable Care Act of 2010
- Hospital mergers, closures, and strategic partnering
- Value-Based Purchasing
- Accountable Care Organizations
- Global caps
- The future of healthcare and healthcare reimbursement

References

Centers for Medicare & Medicaid Services (CMS). (2015). Hospital Value-Based Purchasing. Retrieved from https://www.cms.gov/Medicare/Quality-Initiatives-Patient-Assessment-Instruments/hospital-value-based-purchasing/index.html?redirect=/hospital-value-based-purchasing/

The Henry J. Kaiser Family Foundation. (2015). Key facts about the uninsured population. Retrieved from http://kff.org/uninsured/fact-sheet/key-facts-about-the-uninsured-population/

Kliff, Sarah. (2012). Massachusetts aims for another health care first: A global spending cap. *The Washington Post.* Retrieved from https://www.washingtonpost.com/news/wonk/wp/2012/07/31/massachusetts-aims-for-another-health-care-first-a-global-spending-cap/

Organisation for Economic Co-operation and Development (OECD). (2015). *Health at a glance: How does the United States compare?* Retrieved from http://www.oecd.org/unitedstates/Health-at-a-Glance-2015-Key-Findings-UNITED-STATES.pdf

Smith, J. C., & Medalia, C. (2014). *Health insurance in the United States: 2013 current population reports.* U.S. Department of Commerce, Economics and Statistics Administration, U.S. Census Bureau.

Tandon, A., Murray, C. J. L., Lauer, J. A., & Evans, D. B. (2001). *Measuring overall health system performance for 191 countries.* GPE Discussion Paper Series: No. 30. EIP/GPE/EQC World Health Organization. Retrieved from http://www.who.int/healthinfo/paper30.pdf

10

Governing Boards & Specialty Organizations

A book on budgeting and finance in healthcare isn't really complete without a discussion of governing boards and specialty organizations because boards oversee financial operations of any organization. Healthcare and specialty organizations survive only if they are financially stable. Nurses can be extremely valuable contributors to any hospital or other healthcare facility board and certainly to specialty organizations within the nursing profession. It is also important for nurses to consider appointment to key committees and board positions locally, in their respective states, and at the federal level. Did you ever consider being appointed to a special committee of the president of the United States? You may think that this is impossible, but I have had colleagues who have served in such positions. Nurses bring many attributes to such committees and boards. They understand the relevance of patient care and also the financial aspects of providing that care. Nurses do not live in a vacuum. They are part of a community and as such they know what is going on in healthcare locally, statewide, and nationally. They realize the cost-competitive environment that exists in healthcare right now. Because the healthcare delivery system and the reimbursement models are changing, now is the perfect time for nurses to consider being appointed to such committees and boards.

The purpose of a governing body is just as the name implies: governance. Members of the governing body include the board of directors, chief executive officer (CEO), and nonvoting members like the chief nursing officer (CNO) or chief financial officer (CFO). Governing bodies generally have an executive committee. For example, on a hospital board, the executive committee may consist of the following:

- Chair
- First vice chair
- Second vice chair
- Treasurer
- Secretary

A specialty organization is an organization within the nursing profession that exists to serve members, usually registered nurses, who practice in various specialties of nursing. Two examples are the Emergency Nurses Association (ENA), whose members are nurses working in emergency departments, trauma care, and other similar services. The International Nurses Society on Addictions (IntNSA) serves members who practice in the area of addictions nursing; however, as addictions cross all practice areas, emergency department, medical-surgical units, intensive care units, and other areas, any nurse can join and belong to the organization.

The executive committee of a specialty nursing organization may consist of the following:

- President
- President-elect
- Treasurer
- Secretary

The CEO in most hospitals is a voting board member. The CNO in most hospitals is not a voting board member, but generally attends all board meetings as an invited guest.

The goal of national nursing organizations is to have 10,000 nurses appointed to various types of organizations' boards (AAN, 2015). Examples of some of these organizations include the following:

- Hospital not-for-profit board
- Hospital system/network board
- Hospital foundation board
- Hospital for-profit board
- American Nurses Association board
- American Nurses Credentialing Center board
- State nurses association boards
- Specialty nursing board
- EMS/rescue squad board
- American Heart Association board
- American Red Cross board
- Charitable organization board
- State Peer Assistance board
- And many others

The American Academy of Nursing (AAN) is a founding member of the Nurses on Boards Coalition, a group of national nursing organizations working together to increase nurses' presence on corporate and non-profit health-related boards of directors throughout the country.

Current members of this important coalition include AARP, the American Association of Colleges of Nursing, Sigma Theta Tau International, and many others. Other organizations may certainly choose to be a part of this very important coalition.

Many boards lack an authority on the patient experience, quality, and safety. There are over three million nurses nationally. Nurses have always been the largest component of the healthcare workforce, yet their voices are rarely heard on boards. Nurses also move policy. They can certainly be excellent contributing board members.

One impetus to having nurses on boards is to meet goals established by the landmark Institute of Medicine (IOM) report on the future of nursing published in 2010.

Fiduciary Responsibilities

Governing board members have a fiduciary responsibility, which implies that they are to provide oversight so that the organization maintains fiscal soundness. Governing board members must be honest, ethical, forthright, and objective.

Primary responsibilities of a hospital's governing board include the following:

- Hiring the executive staff to manage and run the day-to-day operations of the facility

- Fiscal accountability
- Final approval on all policies and procedures
- Credentialing of the medical staff and associate medical staff, for example, advanced practice nurses (APNs)
- Quality and safety
- Strategic planning
- Capital improvement projects
- Fundraising
- Community activism
- Major human capital resources decisions (that is, what employees contribute dollar-wise to their health benefits)

NOTE

The primary role of a governing body is oversight, not day-to-day operational management.

Today, hospital and health network/system boards focus on quality and patient safety. Key to improved quality is transparency and accountability. Governing boards have a responsibility for oversight of such initiatives.

Regarding quality, what governing boards want to see and what they provide oversight for are the following:

- A dashboard or scorecard with metrics
- Review of all sentinel events, unexpected occurrences that cause death or serious injury

- Incentive programs for providers in an effort to improve quality
- Culture change in the organization to quality by assuring evidence-informed decision-making
- Encouragement of multiple stakeholder input
- Continuous measurement with a good feedback loop
- Engagement of patients

Primary responsibilities of a specialty organization's board include the following:

- Hiring either a full-time executive director or contracting with a management company to manage the organization
- Fiscal accountability
- Recommending development of policies and procedures as they relate to the organization
- Final approval on all policies and procedures as related to the organization
- Strategic planning
- Fund-raising
- Membership recruitment

Boards of directors have a major impact on where dollars are spent. The fiduciary responsibility of a board is critical. Boards also assure excellent quality initiatives in an organization and also embrace strategic planning and such initiatives. Nurses on boards can contribute significantly to these processes.

I will use myself as an example. I was appointed to the joint hospital boards of a healthcare system a few months ago. This particular healthcare system has 3 hospitals and over 60 outpatient centers and an array of urgent care centers. I serve on the joint hospital boards and also on the quality and safety committee of one of the hospital boards. At a recent board retreat that focused on population health and quality, the corporate chief operating officer and I were speaking during a social event. He advised me that we "really need your input regarding quality and patient safety." It so happened that my mother-in-law was hospitalized that week in another health system. As a nurse and a son-in-law I observed that my mother-in-law was not eating. Oftentimes, the tray was not left in her reach, and no one assisted her with eating, which she required. I thought of all the metrics that we as board members look at on our dashboard. I would venture to guess and almost assure that the hospital my mother-in-law was at also looked at such metrics. But, what about basic care like bathing and feeding? What good is all of the technology if basic nutrition is not met?

So, at the next quality and safety committee board meeting of the system that I serve on I am going to recommend that we do a point prevalence study to see if patients are getting fed. A point prevalence survey is a study that is done at one point in time. I will recommend that managers take an hour or so on one day and survey the nursing units at one meal, such as lunchtime, to see if patients are getting fed or if the food tray is left by their bedside with no one paying attention to see if patients are eating. The dashboard does not list basic items like eating, but these are some of the most important parameters to assess. That is how my experience can contribute to a board as a nurse.

Governing and Specialty Boards

Governing boards consist of the full board and then a further breakdown into strategic committees such as strategic planning, quality and safety, and the finance committee.

Specialty organization boards consist of the full board and then are further broken down into specific task forces such as membership recruitment, fund-raising, and educational programming.

In both types of organizations, ad hoc committees may be appointed to study a special request or circumstance and report back to the board. When the work of the ad hoc committee has been completed, the committee is dissolved.

Term limits and titles vary from organization to organization. In both types of board, bylaws regulate titles and terms of elected/appointed members.

I have had the opportunity to serve on specialty nursing boards in various roles. For example, I was president-elect and president of one of my alma mater's Sigma Theta Tau International chapters. I most recently served 8 years on the International Nurses Society on Addictions Board in various roles: board member, secretary, president-elect, and then president. One could be elected as a board member for two consecutive 2-year terms, and following that one would have to have at least a 1-year hiatus from serving on the board.

The healthcare system board that I serve on is for a 3-year term. Most healthcare organizations have 3-year terms, and one can be reappointed for three or four consecutive terms but then have to leave the board and not serve again. The goal, of course, is to get new blood on the board with new ideas and perspectives.

So, how did I get appointed to the board in the first place? Having attended all board meetings as a nonvoting member when I was a CNO, I always had the idea in the back of my head to serve on a hospital board. Two years ago, I placed this idea on my bucket list. I had the opportunity to have lunch one day with the CEO of one of the hospitals in the healthcare system that I had been appointed to. She is a nurse and a CEO. At the end of our lunch meeting I advised her that my goal was to get appointed to a hospital board. I told her that I would love to do it for her system, but that if she also knew of any other health systems that would perhaps consider a nurse on their board I would be interested. I mentioned this to her because I knew that in her CEO role she had to network with other CEOs and boards. I also expressed my interest to a few other healthcare system executives. It took 2 years of waiting, but this past year I was asked to lunch to meet the chair of the board, the nominating committee chair, and the CEO (the one I originally spoke to). This August I was appointed to the board. When I reflect on this, I think that one of the things you have to do is make others aware of your interest.

Good boards conduct periodic self-evaluations. Hospital boards have generally concluded that long term limits and/or absent term limits of board members should no longer exist.

Some problems with governing boards include the following:

- **Long term limits**
- **Lack of term limits**
- **No rotation of the chairperson**
- **Too many board members:** The larger the board the more difficult to get decisions made and the less

likely that all board members will read and complete all the preparatory work that is necessary to serve on a board.

- **Too few board members:** The major problem here is that there will not be enough members to have quorum for voting if certain members miss board meetings.

- **Lack of commitment of board members:** Being a board member takes time. In not-for-profit organizations these are usually voluntary positions. Some board members just show up to the meeting but do not prep appropriately by reading all of the documents. They then cannot effectively contribute to the meetings.

- **Unfamiliarity with the nature of the organization:** Healthcare is much different than the organization they may work in or own. It is difficult for some board members to understand the complex billing, coding, and financial systems of healthcare.

Conflicts of Interest

A conflict of interest exists every time one has interest in one company and that crosses over to another organization. Conflict of interest generally implies that a person may gain something (usually financially). For example, suppose I own a company that supplies a certain healthcare product. The hospital that I now become a board member at utilizes the healthcare product that the company that I own supplies. Now a potential conflict of interest exists. Legal and ethical issues come to play here because it could be perceived that I am now reaping financial benefits from the hospital board that I serve on.

> ### NOTE
>
> *I have a personal conflict of interest example. I am on a health system board. My daughter who was looking for a new job stated to me one day that she was going to apply to the healthcare system that I am board member at. I advised her that she should not do that, and if she did, I would make certain that she did not get a job there. I told her that she was not going to use my position as a board member to gain employment. She did not apply.*
>
> *I take my position as a board member very seriously and even though my daughter would perhaps make an excellent employee, the perception would be that I got her the job; and I do not want that perception. When people are in such positions, they must have a very strong moral compass. My motto is: "whenever in doubt if a conflict of interest exists, avoid it!"*

Some board members may have a conflict of interest by being on the board. Consider the following example: John J. owned a productive real estate company in the town where the hospital was located. The board sought him to be a board member because the hospital at times would purchase properties near or adjacent to the hospital.

The hospital was very interested in purchasing a parcel of land that would serve as future development for a long-term care facility that the hospital was planning to build near the main facility. John J. worked on the sale of this property. Without the realtor disclosing anything to the board, this was a land flip deal where the hospital paid many thousands more dollars than the fair market price, and the realtor (John J.) benefitted immensely with a huge profit.

The ethical and legal dilemmas in this case are that this board member really padded his own pockets financially.

Although he served the hospital by getting the land that it wanted, he also made a huge profit on the deal and at the hospital's expense. Had he made less of a profit, the hospital would have had more dollars to spend on development of the nursing home. The hospital board did learn from this situation. This board member was eventually terminated. There is no reason why a hospital cannot utilize a real estate agency in the local community, but if the owner of one agency is on the board, it would be more ethical and legal to utilize another agency for land purchases.

TIPS TO AVOID CONFLICTS OF INTEREST

Disclosure: When in doubt, disclose potential conflicts of interest.

Avoidance: Avoid situations where one would personally benefit (especially financially).

Transparency: Be transparent and honest in all interactions.

Moral Compass: Know your own ethical values and moral compass. Have moral courage to do what is right.

Consult: When in doubt if a conflict exists, consult an attorney who can advise you accordingly.

Your Moral Gut: This is what I feel is perhaps most important. If your gut tells you that something just doesn't seem right, then avoid it. Your gut is usually right.

Specialty Organization Budgets

You've read about hospital budgeting in detail throughout this book; this section does not repeat that information by including such budgets in the discussion/examples. Instead, here we consider items that may be included in a budget for a specialty organization.

Sample Specialty Nursing Organization Categories of Revenue and Expenses

In this section, we review the budget components you've become familiar with throughout this book. Therefore, the descriptions here are brief, serving just as a reminder of concepts you've learned earlier.

A specialty nursing organization's financial performance is defined by the following:

- Total assets

- Total liabilities

- Investments

A specialty nursing organization's revenue may derive from any or all of the following:

- **Membership dues:** Some specialty organizations collect dues from members, and this is often an important source of revenue for the organization.

- **Educational offerings:** Programs offered. For example, at the International Nurses Society on Addictions annual conference, one of the members does an Addictions 101 course as a pre-conference. The organization charges a fee for this course.

- **Certification board:** Some organizations offer specialty certification. There is a cost an individual pays to be certified. Other revenue would come from a prep course to be successful on the exam. Again, an organization would charge for the prep course.

- **Journal:** Some organizations publish a journal quarterly, monthly, biannually, etc. They usually contract with a publisher to publish the journal. There is a fee for the journal. For members of the organization, the annual membership dues usually cover the cost of the journal. Revenue made from the journal is allocated to both the publisher and the organization.

- **Products/services:** Many organizations sell mugs, T-shirts, and other items with the organization's logo on the items.

- **Annual conference:** It is rare when a conference generates revenue because it is so expensive to run conferences today. However, some do make revenue, and conferences are a way to gain more members in an organization.

- **Other income:** Other income can result from donations to the organization. Another example would be if the organization wrote a grant and received grant funding.

A specialty nursing organization's expenses may include any or all of the following:

- **Administrative:** This is normally costs of either hiring staff like an executive director or contracting with a management company, which usually charges a monthly fee that is negotiated.

- **Board:** These are board expense items like face-to-face board meetings, travel and hotel accommodations for such meetings, meal expense, and all expenses when a board member attends a conference or program on behalf of the organization.

- **Educational offering:** Cost of program fees for putting on the education program.

- **Journal:** Costs of producing the journal and payment to the editor of the journal. Again, these rates are usually contracted rates.

- **Marketing products/services:** Cost of marketing materials such as printing or purchasing member lists to market products and services to.

- **Annual conference:** Cost of conference space, meals, use of equipment such as sound equipment, LCD projectors, laptops, etc.

- **Other expenses:** Board of directors insurance, travel expense of the executive director, expense if an organization hires consultants such as policy expert, and so on.

Now that you've reviewed the components you must review to determine a specialty organization's financial health/performance, let's look at a sample budget for Organization XYZ, in Figure 10.1.

This budget provides an example of what a specialty organization's budget looks like. You can see here that revenue exceeded expenses, which is the goal of any well-functioning organization.

	2013 ACTUAL	2013 Budget	2014 ACTUAL	2014 Budget	2015 Budget
Income					
Journal Royalty	15,000.00	15,000.00	15,000.00	15,000.00	15,000.00
Conference Income	34,160.12	25,417.00	30,340.00	37,700.00	33,825.00
Investment Income	152.69	25.00	3.05	5.00	5.00
Ad type 1	1,200.00	500.00	3,600.00	1,200.00	3,600.00
Ad type 2	3,075.00	3,500.00	3,170.00	3,000.00	2,375.00
Total Marketing	4,275.00	4,000.00	6,770.00	4,200.00	5,975.00
Membership Dues					
Member type 1	8,265.00	5,130.00	10,024.00	6,650.00	9,400.00
Member type 2	700.00	1,200.00	120.00	0.00	120.00
Member type 3	48,689.50	45,825.00	45,614.00	48,175.00	47,000.00
Member type 4	1,320.00	1,760.00	801.00	660.00	1,100.00
Member type 5	0.00	0.00	1,336.00	600.00	625.00
Total Membership Dues	58,974.50	53,915.00	57,895.00	56,085.00	58,245.00
Sales	485.00	400.00	165.00	450.00	150.00
Total Income	113,047.31	98,757.00	110,173.05	113,440.00	113,200.00
Expense					
Bank Fees	27.70	0.00	0.00	50.00	50.00
Board of Directors					
Awards	590.77	250.00	559.90	750.00	600.00
Gifts	281.10	0.00	199.71	350.00	250.00
Meetings	0.00	1,300.00	640.95	1,300.00	1,500.00
Miscellaneous	575.29	200.00	0.00	0.00	0.00
Staff Travel	1,457.58	950.00	877.10	750.00	1,000.00
Total Board of Directors	2,904.74	2,700.00	2,277.66	3,150.00	3,350.00
Conference Expenses	33,403.58	37,954.00	33,616.56	31,950.00	33,600.00
Credit Card Transactions					
Monthly/Yearly Fees	360.00	0.00	360.00	360.00	360.00

Transaction Fees	1,985.90	1,000.00	2,188.72	2,500.00	2,500.00
Total Credit Card Transactions	2,345.90	1,000.00	2,548.72	2,860.00	2,860.00
Journal Publication	4,241.52	3,000.00	0.00	3,500.00	3,500.00
Legal/Professional Fees					
Accountant	400.00	715.00	0.00	650.00	650.00
Corporate Filings	80.00	0.00	120.00	80.00	150.00
Insurance	2,455.00	1,771.00	3,026.00	2,500.00	3,050.00
Miscellaneous	0.00	0.00	0.00	0.00	100.00
Total Legal/Professional Fees	2,935.00	2,486.00	3,146.00	3,230.00	3,950.00
Management Fee	41,445.00	40,800.00	43,656.00	43,656.00	43,656.00
Office Expenses					
Conference Calls	91.20	150.00	0.00	0.00	0.00
Copies/Printing	342.74	1,150.00	291.32	450.00	300.00
Fax	13.80	0.00	4.40	15.00	10.00
Graphic Design	1,169.50	0.00	985.00	250.00	250.00
Promotional Emails	346.86	498.00	525.00	350.00	550.00
Postage	1,063.18	600.00	211.33	600.00	250.00
Scans	23.40	0.00	69.20	50.00	75.00
Supplies	0.00	250.00	157.00	0.00	0.00
Telephone	305.86	725.00	80.07	325.00	100.00
Web Hosting	3,160.56	1,450.00	559.70	850.00	600.00
Total Office Expenses	6,517.10	4,823.00	2,883.02	2,890.00	2,135.00
Sales Expense	40.28	150.00	0.00	850.00	100.00
Total Expense	93,860.82	92,913.00	88,127.96	92,136.00	93,201.00
Net Income	19,186.49	5,844.00	22,045.09	21,304.00	19,999.00

FIGURE 10.1

Specialty Nursing Organizational Budget for Organization XYZ.

Summary

This chapter covered the following:

- Governing boards and specialty boards
- Conflicts of interest
- Specialty boards categories of revenue and expense
- Specialty organization budgets
- Sample budget of a specialty organization

References

American Academy of Nursing (AAN). (2015). Nurses on boards coalition. Retrieved from http://www.aannet.org/index. php?option=com_content&view=article&id=742:nurses-on-boards-coalition&catid=23:news&Itemid=133

11

QSEN Competencies and High-Reliability Organizations

In October 2005, an ongoing multiphase project known as Quality and Safety Education for Nurses (QSEN) began at the University of North Carolina at Chapel Hill School of Nursing. As obvious from its name, the QSEN project focuses on quality and safety, and nursing contributions to such, in healthcare settings. The QSEN project has subsequently outlined core competencies (consisting of knowledge, skills, and attitudes [KSAs]) that all prelicensure nursing students should master. QSEN competencies have also been developed for graduate nursing students.

Mastery of QSEN core competencies, leading to implementation of them throughout a healthcare system, is likely to result in what is called a high-reliability organization. As you will learn in this chapter, QSEN-style improvement initiatives that result in high reliability lead to improved reimbursement and thus sounder financial health for high-reliability organizations.

Quality and Safety Education for Nurses

The goal of the QSEN project is to improve the quality and safety of healthcare delivered to patients. It involves the translation of the QSEN competencies into practice through identified KSAs. Therefore, obviously, education is a large component of QSEN.

The six core KSAs of QSEN, based on the Institute of Medicine competencies (IOM, 2003), are as follows:

- **Patient-centered care:** Recognizes that the patient is a full partner in the provision of compassionate and coordinated care. This competency addresses the patient's preferences, values, and needs.

- **Teamwork and collaboration:** Recognizes that care is delivered through interprofessional teams. Teamwork and collaboration must utilize open communication, mutual respect, and shared decision-making, with the ultimate goal of improved patient care and quality outcomes.

- **Evidence-based practice (EBP), or what I call evidence-informed practice (EIP):** Recognizes that nurses must integrate the best current evidence with clinical expertise and incorporate patient/family preferences and values in the delivery of optimal patient care.

- **Quality improvement:** Recognizes that the outcomes of care processes are monitored and evaluated with data so that improvement methods are designed, tested, and implemented to continuously improve the quality and safety of patient care delivered in healthcare systems.

- **Safety:** Recognizes that the risk of harm is minimized to patients and providers through system effectiveness and the individual performance of providers.

- **Information technology (informatics):** Recognizes that informatics is used to communicate, improve knowledge, and mitigate error. In addition, it supports clinical, administrative, educational, and research decision-making. Key metrics must be defined by the organization. Data must be mined, and this is made possible by good informatics systems.

QSEN Competencies and Budgeting

So, how do the QSEN competencies relate to financial and budgeting concepts for nurse managers? With the focus on improving quality and controlling costs, a cultural shift or change needs to occur. Nurse managers are held accountable for performance measures and metrics.

The goal in the healthcare delivery system has been to improve quality while at the same time decreasing costs. For nursing, this has been a struggle because a lot of nurse managers believe that improved staffing relates to improved quality. There is a fine line in staffing. Actually if there is too much staff, less tends to get done. If there is too little staff, patient care might not be up to par. Research evidence has demonstrated that the right mix of staff in nursing is critical. For example, those organizations that have a higher RN-to-patient ratio tend to have better outcomes because registered nurses (RNs) are more accountable and can do more than other levels of staff. These same institutions have lower costs.

Consider this, if a patient develops a Stage IV pressure ulcer while in the hospital, what is the associated cost? An organization also may not be paid for iatrogenic events that develop within the organization. Often, such events lead to prolonged hospital stays and treatment that are not even reimbursable today. There is a definite link of quality to risk management and costs. Generally, the lower the quality, the higher the potential of risk to the organization, which ultimately ties to higher costs.

Improved quality ties to improved outcomes, which ultimately leads to more satisfied patients and lower costs. There is a direct link between patient satisfaction and finance. The Hospital Consumer Assessment of Healthcare Providers and Systems (HCAHPS) scores today tie to hospital reimbursement. For instance, 30% of the revenue under Medicare results from an organization achieving certain patient satisfaction scores. The other 70% of reimbursement ties to the process of care (Adamy, 2012). This results in more of an algorithm approach to patient care.

For example, a 55-year-old male enters the hospital emergency department with chest pain. The standard of care is the algorithm. The patient will have vital signs taken. An intravenous line will be inserted. An ECG will be done. Lab work, including cardiac enzymes and troponin levels, will be done. A portable chest X-ray will be done. The patient will be administered aspirin if appropriate, as well as nitroglycerin and morphine. The patient will receive supplemental oxygen if the patient's oxygen saturation of room air is less than 94%. Should the ECG be positive for a myocardial infarction, the patient will be transported promptly to the cardiac catheterization lab for PCI (percutaneous cardiac intervention, that is, angioplasty and stent placement). Should any step in this process be omitted, less reimbursement will be received because the process of care was not followed explicitly.

Incentivizing Quality

Why is there concern about compliance, outcomes, and reimbursement? Consider the following information from the Centers for Medicare & Medicaid Services (CMS, 2013):

- The dollar amount per capita spent on healthcare in the United States exceeds that of any other nation in the world. Because the United States has an entrepreneurial healthcare system, administrative costs are much higher in the United States as compared to other countries.

- Healthcare costs are a significant portion of the gross national product (GNP) and the gross domestic product (GDP).

- Hospital care (both inpatient and outpatient care) is the most significant service with higher costs.

What has driven QSEN and changes in the reimbursement system for healthcare services?

- Adverse patient outcomes, many of which are preventable

- Public perception of the quality of healthcare in the United States

Examples of adverse patient outcomes include the following:

- Wrong-site surgery

- Wrong medication

- Prescribing errors

- Transcribing errors

- Poor communication (both written and verbal). This usually is one of the major problems in adverse outcomes.

- Healthcare-associated infections (HAIs)

> **NOTE**
>
> *The Institute of Medicine (IOM) report* Crossing the Quality Chasm *highlighted in 2001 the tens of thousands of iatrogenic events and deaths that occur in U.S. healthcare systems on an annual basis (IOM, 2001). Even more recently, a study in the* Journal of Patient Safety *reported in 2013 that between 210,000 and 440,000 patients each year die from iatrogenic effects after presenting themselves in a healthcare setting (James, 2013).*

The federal Centers for Medicare & Medicaid Services (CMS) and private healthcare insurers recognize that increasing costs and poor-quality outcomes are not improving. One way to improve these two indicators is via financial incentives to reward good quality and to penalize poor quality. Voluntary agencies such as the following are also driving initiatives to improve care:

- **The Leapfrog Group:** The Leapfrog Group is arguably the premiere nonprofit watchdog group that focuses on transparency in healthcare, which they believe will lead to more informed consumers and better outcomes across the board.

- **U.S. News & World Report:** Ranks hospitals both nationally and regionally on an annual basis for the quality of care and the services provided. Ranks individual specialties such as neuro, ortho, cardiac, etc.

- **Hospital Safety Score:** Grades hospitals on how safe they keep their patients from errors, injuries, accidents, and infections.

- **Consumer Reports:** Hospital ratings designed to assist the consumer compare hospitals based on patient safety scores, the patient experience, patient outcomes, and certain hospital practices.

- **National Quality Forum (NQF):** Nonprofit membership organization that promotes patient protections and healthcare quality through measurement and public reporting. Provides research recommendations designed to improve healthcare quality.

A few regulating and accrediting agencies even mandate the incentivization of quality, as follows:

- **DNV:** A global certification body that works with healthcare organizations around the world to minimize risk and maximize opportunities for excellence through safety and quality. For more information about the DNV, see http://dnvglhealthcare.com/

- **The Joint Commission (TJC):** A voluntary organization that accredits and certifies healthcare facilities and programs for quality. The goal of TJC is to improve quality care for patients. For more information about the TJC, see http://www.jointcommission.org/about_us/about_the_joint_commission_main.aspx

- **Respective State Departments of Health:** State departments of health also conduct health facility evaluations. How this is conducted will vary from each state. For example, one state my survey every healthcare facility once annually. Another state may accept one of the voluntary certifications/accreditations and only do a site visit if there is a specific patient complaint. Surveys with state departments of health are involuntary as these entities grant licensure to healthcare facilities so that they can operate in a respective state. For more information, see a respective state department of health website.

Value-based incentives include the following:

- Transparency (Consumers can select healthcare facilities and systems based on quality and performance as well as cost.)

- More bundled payments for services rendered

- Hospital readmission program

- Hospital inpatient value-based purchasing program

- Hospital-acquired conditions program

Traditionally, payment was usually made per individual for healthcare services provided. Healthcare organizations were profitable under such a system. Now, however, no payment is made for illnesses and problems caused by the healthcare system (iatrogenesis). However, rewards are available for good-quality outcomes.

Medicare bills under the Diagnosis Related Group (DRG) system for inpatient acute care hospitalization. This is a form of bundled payment; a case rate is utilized rather than per diem charges. Under the Patient Protection and Affordable Care Act (PPACA, or just ACA), a bundle may include only one payment per event or one payment per patient per year to an accountable care organization (ACO), thus creating a form of capitated payment.

Hospital value-based purchasing programs have also been developed. These entail the following:

- Payment for care beyond just the volume of care delivered

- Payment for care that rewards better value, patient outcomes, and innovation

- Evaluation of performance that gets added into the payment system

Hospital value-based purchasing programs, as shown in Figure 11.1, typically receive payment as follows:

- 70% of the payment comes from the clinical process of care

- 30% of the payment comes from the patient experience as measured by the HCAHPS scores

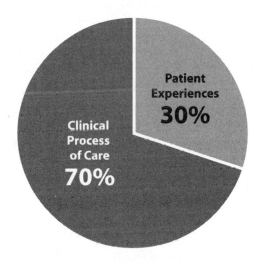

FIGURE 11.1
*Reimbursement Model Under
Hospital Value-Based Purchasing Program.*

The Clinical Process of Care

As mentioned earlier, the clinical process of care typically follows an algorithmic approach. For example, with a suspected acute coronary syndrome patient, certain care processes must be implemented to achieve the 70% reimbursement mark.

- ECG

- Portable chest X-ray

- Labs such as cardiac enzymes, troponin levels, chemistry profile, CBC, INR

- MONA (morphine, oxygen, nitroglycerin and aspirin) therapy. Remember that the acronym comprises the steps in treatment, but not the order in which you perform them.

- If positive for myocardial infarction, fibrinolytic therapy within 30 minutes of arrival to the emergency department (ED) or percutaneous cardiac intervention (PCI) within 90 minutes of arrival to the ED

The Patient Experience

The patient experience is evaluated based on a number of factors, including the following:

- Measured by HCAHPS scores

- Dimensions are outlined

- Nurse communication

- Physician communication

- Hospital staff responsiveness

- Pain management

- Medication management

- Hospital cleanliness

- Discharge information

- Overall hospital rating

A point measure gets assigned to each measure or dimension. Rates are compared for the performance period against the baseline period.

> **NOTE**
>
> *HCAHPS scores are valuable because public reporting enhances accountability in healthcare. It makes transparent the quality of hospital care provided in return for investment by the public.*

The Role of Nursing

Nursing-sensitive value-based purchasing seeks to optimize staffing and the healthcare practice environment through outcome incentives and transparency of structure, process, and patient outcome measures. This initiative:

- Establishes core measures
- Improves HCAHPS overall scores
- Improves hospital value-based purchasing scores
- Impacts Medicare reimbursement to the hospital
- Recognizes the criticality of nursing to improved quality of patient care

The following list identifies nursing areas and concepts that have been proven to work to improve the safety and quality of patient care:

- Safe staffing
- Higher RN staffing—generally, 75% of staff should be RNs
- Teamwork
- Trust
- Accountability
- Transparency
- Exceptional nursing leadership

You might at this point be wondering how all of this relates to QSEN competencies. The following list identifies how:

- Cost savings can be achieved when adverse events are decreased.

- Cost savings can be achieved when hospital readmissions are prevented.

- Nursing is critical to the reductions of adverse patient events and hospital readmissions.

- Nurses spend the most time with the patient, thus improving the quality of nursing care is crucial.

The following factors related to the structure of nursing care impact outcomes:

- Supply of nursing staff

- Skill level of nursing staff

- Education of nursing staff

- Certification of nursing staff

Nursing care should seek to provide optimal care while also avoiding HAIs. Several processes help to avoid them, as follows:

- Good handwashing helps avoid HAIs by removing bacteria from one's hands prior to touching a patient, thus preventing cross contamination.

- Proper sterilization of instruments, which prevents infections secondary to procedures.

- Proper refrigeration of food to prevent foodborne illnesses.

- Judicious use of antibiotics in order to prevent resistance patterns of bacteria and other organisms.

Nursing care has an impact on the following, which are also all factors that are evaluated in an outcome-incentivized scheme:

- Prevention of infections: SSIs (surgical site infections), VAP (ventilator-associated pneumonia), CAUTIs (community-acquired urinary tract infections)

- Prevention of decubitus ulcers: Stages III and IV

- Prevention of falls and falls with injury

- Length of stay in the ICU

- Readmissions

Nursing care is critical to financial reimbursement and thus to the entire budgeting system of any healthcare organization or system:

- Reimbursement is based on bundled billing.

- Reimbursement is based on the achievement of clinical indicators and the patient experience.

- Nursing is critical to this process.

- Nursing-sensitive indicators are critical.

- Nursing is critical to the provision of excellent patient care.

- Quality of nursing care is crucial to hospital survival.

A Final Word on Incentive-Based Reimbursement

FIGURE 11.2
Total performance score = Reimbursement.

Another way to view this is: No outcome, no payment.

Population Health

In my experience, the United States has primarily focused on quality in hospitals. Now, though, more and more care is rendered in a variety of settings outside of hospitals. Population health is becoming vitally important in achieving excellent quality outcomes for patients.

Population health refers to caring for individuals in a community so that they maintain optimum health. Population health involves key metrics about the community served.

POPULATION HEALTH IN ACTION

A quality-improvement team in an acute care hospital decided to visit a community that they were caring for. In some of the elder homes, the bathrooms (in particular, the bathtubs) did not have shower bars, and therefore the risk of falling for this population was great. The hospital offered to pay to have shower bars installed in all bathrooms of those in the community who did not already have them.

Home Care

Home care is a critical component of an ACO. Insurance companies will pay for home care services because generally these services are less costly than hospital admissions and can even prevent hospital admissions.

Recently, a new rating system for the evaluation of home care services was released by the Centers for Medicare

& Medicaid Services (CMS). Ratings are based on specific criteria. The criteria utilized focus on the quality of patient care and the skill of practitioners providing home care services. The system designed by CMS is known as Home Health Compare (HHC). Home care agency scores should empower the public to select the home care agency that can better serve their needs.

Home care services generally include the following:

- Skilled nursing care

- Nursing aide care

- Nutritional services

- Rehabilitation services

- Social services

Under the CMS evaluation criteria, the CMS uses two different methods to assess home care agencies. One method evaluates statistical reports from the respective home care agency about staff treatment of patients and patient improvement. The second method relies on data from patient surveys (that is, the patient experience with home care services). Nine specific areas are evaluated. The types of services assessed include the following:

- Care provided to patients in a timely manner

- Information and education on drugs were provided

- Flu vaccines were administered during the flu season

- How often a patient improved ambulation

- How frequently a patient would get in and out of bed

- How frequently the patient could bathe himself or herself

- Was the patient able to perform activities with less pain?

- Was the patient able to perform activities with less shortness of breath?

- How often the patient required acute care hospitalization

The highest rating that a home care agency can achieve is a five-star rating.

The five top-rated states first time around were the following:

- California

- Florida

- Rhode Island

- Utah

- New Jersey (Leonard, 2015)

As you can clearly understand from this discussion, the CMS and the federal government are most concerned with the quality of care that patients receive, the patient experience, and the patients' evaluation of such.

High-Reliability Organizations: Rocket Science or Common Sense?

One major force that has been driving quality-improvement initiatives in hospitals is the Institute of Medicine (IOM). The IOM's report *To Err Is Human* (IOM, 1999), which laid out in graphic numbers the shocking scale of iatrogenic events (that is, what health providers cause), has driven quality improvement in hospitals. Although improvement efforts have been made and demonstrated, completely eradicating human error is nearly impossible. The reality is that human beings make mistakes, and medicine (as well as nursing) is not an exact science. In an effort to prevent human error, hospitals are now embarking on what is termed *high reliability*. The goal is to consistently and to continuously provide high levels of safety and quality across all healthcare services and settings.

The Goals of High Reliability

The goal of high-reliability science, as it is called, is to standardize processes so that the variability in outcomes is eliminated. According to Chassin and Loeb (2013), healthcare organizations need to make three major changes:

- Commitment of leadership: This includes the board, senior management, senior physicians, and nurse leaders

- Incorporation of all principles and practices that contribute to the creation of a culture of safety within the organization

- Adoption and widespread deployment of the most effective process-improvement tools and methods

Healthcare organizations have tended to follow a reactive approach to quality (i.e., trying to improve the quality after a major negative event has occurred). Creation of a high-reliability culture is a proactive stance that navigates an organization from high quality to high reliability. The processes that create workflow inefficiencies need to be evaluated, and new processes that eliminate such inefficiencies need to be employed. The goal is to drive processes that result in an absolute minimum number of errors. Some organizations are targeting *zero* errors. This zero target might be unrealistic, though, because the human factor is always present.

Getting There

One key aspect in attaining high reliability is creating the intersection of safety and transparency. The following list identifies some of the key principles necessary to create such an intersection:

- Create a culture of transparency, safety, and quality that involves a continuous learning process.

- Institute action-oriented reviews that comprehensively evaluate safety performance data.

- Create a culture of caring that encourages everyone to be transparent so that problems can be identified and action taken to prevent future incidents.

- Institute peer review so that the performance of everyone is continuously evaluated.

- Stamp out disruptive behaviors and substandard performance.

- Raise the performance bar so that everyone in the organization continually tries to improve himself or herself as well as others.

- Be collaborative.

- Be transparent in reporting performance to regulators and other agencies.

QSEN provides the KSAs that should foster high reliability so that errors are minimized and potentially eliminated. Such proactive improvement initiatives can only contribute to improved reimbursement and financial improvement and, most important, satisfied patients. It is not rocket science that satisfied customers and positive word-of-mouth reporting encourage other patients to access services. Therefore, initiatives that result in that kind of satisfaction can only positively contribute to the sustained growth of a healthcare organization.

Summary

This chapter covered the following:

- The QSEN project and its aims
- How to incentivize quality improvement
- The role the clinical process, the patients, and nurses play in quality improvement
- Population health and home care
- The goal of high reliability

References

Adamy, J. (2012). U.S. ties hospital payments to making patients happy. *The Wall Street Journal*. Retrieved from http://www.wsj.com/articles/SB10000872396390443890304578010264156073132

Centers for Medicare & Medicaid Services (CMS). (2013). Historical national health expenditure data. Retrieved from https://www.cms.gov/research-statistics-data-and-systems/statistics-trends-and-reports/nationalhealthexpenddata/nationalhealthaccountshistorical.html

Chassin, M. R., & Loeb, J. M. (2013). High-reliability health care: Getting there from here. *The Milbank Quarterly, 91*(3), 459-490.

Institute of Medicine (IOM). (1999). *To err is human: Building a safer health system*. Washington, DC: National Academies Press.

Institute of Medicine (IOM). (2001). *Crossing the quality chasm: A new health system for the 21st century*. Washington, DC: National Academies Press.

Institute of Medicine (IOM). (2003). *Health professions education: A bridge to quality*. Washington, DC: National Academies Press.

James, John T. (2013). A new, evidence-based estimate of patient harms associated with hospital care. *Journal of Patient Safety,* 9(3), 122-128.

Leonard, N. (2015). New Jersey's home health agencies score well with federal government. *The Press of Atlantic City.* Retrieved from http://www.pressofatlanticcity.com/news/new-jersey-s-home-health-agencies-score-well-with-federal/article_8edaa80e-3d66-11e5-abbe-7f3bd2a873a1.html

12

Conclusions

As you've learned from this book, financial prudence/
management is the responsibility of everyone who works in
a healthcare setting. Nurse managers, as part of that setting,
are crucial to managing an organization's resources.

The reality is that decreasing reimbursement from all
sectors is likely to be the norm for the foreseeable future.
Because nursing is the largest department in most healthcare
organizations, nurses are in a pivotal position to control
costs. Indeed, nursing budgets generally comprise about
50% or more of an organization's overall budget.

Of course, human capital is by far the greatest expense
in a nursing budget. Controlling labor costs is one of the
most fiscally prudent things a nurse manager can do. This
can be achieved by doing the following:

- Staffing to meet the budgeted nursing hours per
  patient day

- Minimizing overtime expenditures

- Questioning whether a unit really needs additional
  personnel

- Not filling vacated positions unless absolutely
  necessary

To accomplish this, nurse managers must review current work processes. For example, you might explore whether the change of shift report could be shortened in some way so that it does not involve overtime hours (and by extension, overtime dollars). In addition, nurse managers might consider whether supplies could be managed more judiciously.

> **NOTE**
>
> *Every time a supply is overused, people generally think it is no big deal. After all, it's only a few supplies! But you must think differently. What if every department within the organization were overutilizing supplies? That would cause a significant impact in dollars to the entire organization.*

But those aren't the only things nurse managers should do to improve the finances of their organization. Following are five key action points to help nurse managers improve the bottom line for their organization and for healthcare in general. Please review these and assess what you can do in your organization.

Key Action Point 1: Get Politically Involved

My mother always said that *politics* was a bad word. Over the years, though, I have learned that we all must use politics to benefit ourselves and our organizations.

Specifically, nurse managers must be aligned with their organization and their chief executive officer (CEO) with respect to politics that affect reimbursement to the organization. It is vital that nurse managers unite with their CEOs as they try to secure more funding for the delivery of health services.

Without adequate funding, many hospitals are doomed to failure. Does that affect nurses? Absolutely, it does. Think about it: What would happen to you if *your* healthcare organization closed? Where would you seek employment? Even if your hospital were to remain open, what about salary raises? Salary raises cannot occur without adequate funding.

UNDERSTANDING THE ROLE OF PACS

Most CEOs belong to the American Hospital Association (AHA) and their respective state hospital association (for example, the New Jersey Hospital Association [NJHA]). Large organizations like these, as well as the American Nurses Association (ANA), AARP, and others, have political action committees (PACs). Funds donated to these PACs are used to survey political candidates running for office. PACs then make recommendations to the membership of their associations as to who to vote for in upcoming elections.

The take-home message is to get involved—at a grass-roots level, at the state level, and at the federal level. All these levels have a role in funding healthcare.

Write, call, or email your state and federal representatives and urge them to support legislation that funds healthcare and that provides more choice and help with regard to insurance plans to uninsured individuals. The reality is that these representatives do listen. They are there to represent us, and we need to make our issues known to them.

> **NOTE**
>
> *Of course, you should also be a registered voter. Otherwise, what is in it for the politicians who seek your vote?*

Key Action Point 2: Know What Types of Insurance Plans Reimburse Your Organization

Nurse managers must become familiar with the types of insurance products available in the geographic area in which they practice and work. If you aren't sure what types of products are out there, check with someone in your finance department who handles the insurance contracts. Finance can tell you which insurance companies, state programs, and federal programs reimburse your organization, and even break it down by percentage.

When I was a chief nursing officer (CNO), Medicare reimbursement accounted for about 55% of our total reimbursement. Medicare tends not to reimburse as well as some other insurers, so we had to carry other insurers that reimbursed at a higher level to make up the difference. Things were even more difficult for another hospital about 90 miles away that served a large retirement community. In its case, 90% of revenue was from Medicare. As a result, this facility had to manage dollars even more judiciously because their reimbursement was lower than most.

Why must nurse managers understand this? Because reimbursement money is not a bottomless pit. Suppose, for example, that Medicare reimbursements were reduced by 4% in the next fiscal year. Suppose further that your hospital's reimbursement from Medicare averages around $100,000,000 in a given year. A 4% reduction on

$100,000,000 would equate to a $4,000,000 reduction in reimbursement. You might think a $4,000,000 reduction is not terribly significant on a $100,000,000 budget, but what if the CEO had approved a 4% across-the-board raise? How would the CEO meet that obligation when the major form of reimbursement to the organization has just been cut by 4%?

My point is that to construct and understand budgets, a nurse manager must have an understanding of the big picture. Budgets are structured on projected patient volume and the type and amount of reimbursement for those patients.

Key Action Point 3: Develop Strategic Relationships with Key Individuals in Your Organization

It did not take me long to realize that the chief financial officer (CFO) of the hospital had as much or even more clout than the CEO. Think about it: The CFO holds the purse strings to the hospital. This person is responsible for making sure the hospital operates in the black (that is, has a positive bottom line). It follows, then, that nurse managers must establish an excellent relationship with the CFO and other key personnel in their organization's finance department.

Other key personnel in the finance department know "the nuts and bolts about finance." These individuals assist in creating the budgets for the organization. Some of these individuals negotiate managed care contracts. Others create the patient bill from what occurred during the patient's hospital stay. These individuals can assist a nurse manager in gaining a better understanding about finance, reimbursement, managed care, and billing.

As for me, I worked to bond with the CFO of my organization so that he would support me. One day, he asked me to play golf with him in the hospital golf tournament. Anyone who knows me is well aware of the fact that I despise golf. I feel there's no purpose to it. However, because I could see the value in our spending time together on the links, I agreed to play golf with him. I even had a physician colleague mentor me for 10 days prior to the tournament so that I would at least be able to hit the ball in the right direction.

As a manager, you must reach out to others in your organization. You must understand where they are coming from. You must work closely with them. You must engage in Politics 101. That is, you must know and understand the politics of the organization and make them work to your benefit. It is critical that nurses understand and learn this basic skill of navigating organizational politics. You want others to serve the nursing department. That only happens when you have positive working relationships in which everyone tries to work with and understand each other.

Key Action Point 4: Speak the Language of Finance

Before delving into the subject of actually speaking the language of finance, let's review a few communication processes.

Communication Is Vital

Communication is critical to the success of any organization. Just like blood is critical to keeping our cells alive through hemoglobin and the binding of oxygen, communication can be considered the lifeblood of any organization.

Communication can occur in an upward manner (for example, from subordinate to manager), in a downward manner (for example, from manager to subordinate), and in a way that is called lateral communication (that is, communication with others across the organization).

Communication Processes

Communication consists of a number of processes, and at each step of each process miscommunication is a risk. So, to ensure effective, comprehensive, and accurately understood communication, you want to remain mindful of these processes, both from a sender and a receiver perspective.

The sender:

First, the sender of a message needs to have an idea about what to communicate.

Second, the sender of the message needs to frame the idea into some format that can be communicated (for example, an email message, a letter, or a verbal message).

Third, the sender then must actually send the message. This can occur in a variety of formats (verbally, written via interdepartmental mail, or electronically through texting and email).

The receiver:

First, the receiver has to actually receive the message.

Second, the receiver has to review the message.

And, third he or she has to perceive and interpret what the message is saying.

Avoiding Miscommunication

Because the communication process is complex, a problem can occur in any of the previously described steps of communication.

A lot of communication today occurs through email. The missing piece here is the nonverbal cues that you can observe when speaking face-to-face with another person.

Regarding financial management, communication should be done face-to-face and electronically for sharing financial reports so that individuals can review the reports prior to meeting about them.

Today, face-to-face communication does not necessarily mean that the individuals communicating need to be in the same room. Much face-to-face communication is now being done through telecommunication systems such as Skype and Zoom.

It is important to understand what the components of communication are because it is necessary to communicate clearly with both staff and administration in communicating financial performance.

PUTTING FINANCIAL PRINCIPLES IN ACTION

A chief nursing officer (CNO) wanted his nurse managers to gain a better understanding of financial reports so that they could better control expenses, especially overtime. Every 2 weeks the hospital's payroll with associated financial reports would run on a Tuesday. The chief nursing officer, the budget manager from the finance department, and the nurse managers met on Wednesday the day after the reports ran. This went on for about a 6-month time period. The nurse managers learned how to interpret these reports. With applying the principles learned, overtime at this institution was reduced significantly through prudent action of the nursing management staff.

Talk the Talk

One of my biggest concerns as a new CNO was my weakness in finance. It was not that I did not know how to manage a budget. That was not the problem. I can be very frugal with someone else's dollars. I had also had financial-management courses in college. The problem was that I wasn't familiar with key financial terms: amortization, zero-based budgeting, and so on.

The fact is, different departments in different organizations speak different languages. Take nursing as an example. Look at our language—the abbreviations we use, and even the slang. A lot of people have no clue what we are talking about.

If you want to bond with key members of the finance department, you must learn and speak the language of finance. This sage advice was shared with me by one of my professors when I was getting my master's degree in nursing administration, and this advice can take a nurse manager far. By being able to talk the talk, nurse managers will not only gain the respect of the finance department but will also gain clout to get the resources they need for their department.

Think about it: Would you want a surgeon operating on you if he did not know what a scalpel was? This holds true for finance. If you do not understand financial terminology, the finance department will get the impression you do not know what you are doing with the budget. My advice: Memorize key financial terms and gain a better understanding of their meaning. Then, use these terms on a daily basis with key administrators and finance personnel.

Key Action Point 5: Do It

Just as a pianist masters his craft by continuously practicing the piano, to really grasp the meaning of finance, you must practice it. That means doing the following:

- Getting comfortable with reviewing financial reports

- Working with finance to provide reports that you can interpret easily

- Taking an active role, not a passive role, in the preparation of the budget

- Questioning things in the process of creating the budget with finance

Most important, you should monitor budget performance. Compare actual expenses to budgeted expenses. For example, if the aggregate numbers look good, overall expenses were under budget, and patient volume was down, but overtime was increased for the RN staff, ask why. If this was unnecessary overtime, correct it and make sure it does not happen in the next time period. The key is to take corrective action where warranted based on the financial reports and statistics.

One way to get comfortable with the budget and the analysis of the budget is to have the finance budget manager meet with you when financial reports are generated. This person can go over the reports with you and can assist you in better controlling the budget. For example, when I was a CNO, I received financial reports every 2 weeks, when payroll ran. Every time that happened, I met with the finance budget manager and all my administrative directors and nurse managers for an hour or so to go over these reports. The purpose of the meeting was not to embarrass or correct anyone. Rather, it was to help the administrative directors and nurse managers understand the budget reports and what action they needed to take going forward.

To motivate my staff, the finance budget manager and I gave an award at each meeting to the manager who best managed his or her budget. This instilled competition between the nurse managers to try to make their units the best. After about 2 months of doing this, the units were running much more efficiently because the nurse managers really understood the budget, the budget reports, and how to take corrective action to manage within the confines of the budget.

Embracing Change

If you think about it, these five points have really highlighted the need for all nurse managers to embrace the change process as it relates to finance and budgeting.

Social scientist Kurt Lewin described three steps to the change process (Huber, 2013):

   Step 1: Unfreezing

   Step 2: Movement

   Step 3: Refreezing

Step 1: Unfreezing

Step 1 is the unfreezing stage. In this step, you gather data and accurately diagnose the problem. Then you make a decision as to whether a change is needed. You also then need to make others aware of the need for change. The motivation for change should begin in this stage.

Regarding financial reporting and data, nurse managers today must manage fiscally sound units. Controlling expenses is necessary, while the provision of quality care is paramount. Trying to achieve this goal often involves the change process. Examples of this would be implementing a new staffing model of care delivery that better controls costs as well as improves quality. One type of model would be primary care that incorporates patient care techs so that patients' basic needs are met in a more timely manner. Another example would be an electronic health record that documents care being rendered in a more timely manner as well as improves legibility of the medical record.

Step 2: Movement

Step 2 is the movement phase. This is where you develop a formal plan. You formulate goals and objectives. You identify areas of support and resistance.

It is important to include everyone who will be affected by the change in the planning process. Individuals are more apt to buy into change when they are part of the change process.

When you look at the budget and fiscal management, nursing staff must be involved so that they know the goals and objectives of the unit. Everyone has to gain a sense of fiscal awareness. Nurses are critical to patients being satisfied and to achieving good care outcomes. They need to be made aware of what types of reports will be viewed and what action will be taken if, for example, a variance exists.

In this stage, appropriate strategies for implementation of the change are developed. It is important that nurse managers are available to support others through the change process and to offer encouragement as needed.

Nurse managers need to consider strategies for overcoming resistance to the change. For example, nurse managers may need to explain why overtime must be utilized judiciously and that a demonstrated need for overtime must be made prior to their assigning such overtime hours.

Step 3: Refreezing

Step 3 is defined as the refreezing stage. In this stage, the change becomes a permanent part of the organization. It is important that the nurse manager still remain available to support others so that the change remains in place.

During this stage, the change is evaluated. The nurse manager and the staff need to be open to adjusting what was implemented if problems are identified. This will occur through review of financial reports.

You may need to adjust staffing levels. For example, additional registered nurses may need to be employed to provide a higher RN-to-patient ratio. The educational level of the staff may need to be addressed (for example, you may need more master's prepared nurses depending on the acuity of your patients). The key is that the staff and the nurse manager plan strategies and remain open to revisions when necessary so that optimal patient care can be provided in a cost-effective environment.

In Closing

I hope this book has provided you with some tools and ideas for embracing the financial aspect of your organization, your own unit(s), the budget process, and most important, monitoring and managing the budget.

As mentioned, when I became a CNO, one of my biggest fears was finance. But after learning the budget process in depth, I found finance and budgeting to be the most enjoyable part of my job. It was challenging and rewarding to see positive results when I managed the budget and finances correctly.

One of my favorite sports is swimming (not golf). So, I will conclude by encouraging you to take the plunge! Dive into the waters of finance.

References
Huber, D. L. (2013). *Leadership & nursing care management (5th ed.)*. St. Louis, MO: Elsevier.

Index

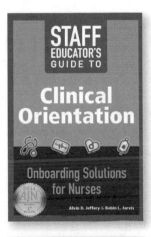

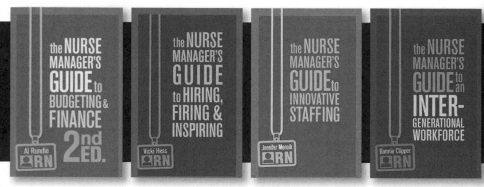